Janet Morley is a freelance writer, speaker and workshop leader. She has worked for Christian Aid and for the Methodist Church, and is the author of several books of prayers and poems, including *All Desires Known, Bread of Tomorrow, The Heart's Time* and *Haphazard by Starlight*, all published by SPCK.

OUR LAST AWAKENING

Poems for living in the face of death

Janet Morley

First published in Great Britain in 2016

Society for Promoting Christian Knowledge
36 Causton Street
London SW1P 4ST
www.spck.org.uk

British Library Cataloguing-in-Publication Data
A catalogue record for this book is available from the British Library

ISBN 978–0–281–07354–2

Typeset by Graphicraft Limited, Hong Kong

Produced on paper from sustainable forests

In memory of Alison, and all my beloved dead

Contents

Contents

Actual crisis

Contents

Immediate grief

Remembering and celebrating

Hope

Contents

Introduction

————◆◆◆————

Bring us, Lord our God,
at our last awakening,
into the house and gate of heaven,
to enter into that gate,
and dwell in that house,
where there shall be
no darkness nor dazzling
but one equal light;
no noise nor silence,
but one equal music;
no fears nor hopes,
but one equal possession;
no ends nor beginnings,
but one equal eternity;
in the habitation of your glory and dominion,
world without end, Amen.

When we think about dying, when we can bear to, it is easy to assume that it involves an increasingly gloomy process of journeying towards the dark. But there are some quite other ways of envisaging what it means to die, as this resonant quotation from a sermon by John Donne in the seventeenth century makes clear. It has been shaped into a prayer that is often used in contemporary funeral services, and it dwells on the prospect of 'our last awakening'. Donne's prayer displays a conviction about the reality of death, not as personal annihilation or as a time of fearful pain or judgement, but the opportunity to awake into a kind of life that is unimaginably more glorious than the dearly loved life we already know. There is a wonderful sense of balance, equality and self-possession in the way Donne envisages the life of heaven.

No doubt Donne was referring to the general resurrection that he believed would take place for all humanity, after their last sleep of earthly death. But I think the phrase 'our last awakening' can also helpfully be applied to the insight and enlightenment that can accompany a willingness to contemplate with an open heart the mortality that we all share, whatever our beliefs about the hereafter. In our own age, Christians may feel as uncertain as anyone else about what that means, or whether it even exists.

Why is poetry helpful in exploring our mortality?

It is frequently said that our modern culture is unwilling to talk or to reflect about death, but in fact poets both ancient and modern, and both Christian and non-Christian, do explore aspects of our mortality in a great deal of depth and detail. I believe there are a number of reasons why poetry is deeply helpful in addressing a subject that concerns us all but which we might usually try to avoid.

- *It is not all morbid and gloomy.* You will find in this book poems with a huge range of tone, from joyful and ecstatic to gentle, ironic, despairing, and even hilarious. Facing death, accompanying the dying, celebrating those who have died, and articulating hope about what lies beyond involves us in experiencing the whole range of human emotions about what it means to live, and to love and be loved.

- *Poets are good at noticing key details.* There is something deeply comforting for those dealing with a terminal diagnosis or suffering acute bereavement in discovering that someone else has been through the experience and observed the particular, unexpected thoughts, insights and feelings that can arise at these times. And for those who have not experienced these things, it can reduce fear to discover that there may be unexpected blessings ahead of us: new perspectives on life, an appreciation of the importance of people not previously noticed, the awareness of our own resilience or a heightened awareness of how precious the earth is.

- *Poets give us permission to name and acknowledge feelings we may be ashamed of.* Grief is often discovered to consist of a range and mixture of very different feelings, and not just dignified sadness or pain as we might imagine. Anger, fear, denial, numbness, gruesome fantasy: all may need to be recognized and named before acceptance is possible. It is helpful to have these things articulated, and not just the truths we wish we believed.

- *Poems are short, but work at lots of levels.* There is something very manageable about the size and shape of a short poem, particularly when we have neither time nor patience to reflect on rational arguments. They tend to be concrete in their observations of the landscape of mortality and grief, and they have a distinct shape and rhythm that gives something firm for the reader to lay hold on. At the same time, they normally work at several different levels. They are able to embrace the paradoxes that are a feature of the terrain, and to hold together different tracks of reality that may be experienced simultaneously. And they may have different insights to offer at different stages of life.

Using this book

It is unlikely that you will want to read this book quickly, or necessarily in the order that the poems are set out (which is also the order in which the commentaries were written). It could be used as a Lent book, reading one poem and commentary a day. But it is more likely to be helpful as something to browse and dip into according to interest or need, depending on where you are in your life and which aspects of reflecting on mortality are most salient for you just now.

The tone and the approach of the poems selected are very varied, and they have been grouped into six broad sections, which explore different feelings about mortality, and different stages of fear, grief, acceptance, celebration and hope.

Ordinary mortality

It is one of the chief conditions under which we live on this earth that our lives are not for ever. This is a fact that connects us with the whole of creation. The cycle of birth, growth, blossoming, ripeness, decay and death is ubiquitous and necessary. It is all right, and we should live recognizing this and making choices that take the ordinariness of our mortality into account. Not to do so, especially as we grow older, is to live in denial and unreality.

Fears and fantasies

We are the only creatures who can foresee our own deaths, even when we are currently perfectly well. We are naturally curious about something about which we can know nothing whatever for certain. We entertain fears, even if we believe that there is nothing the other side of death. We indulge in fantasies about how it might actually feel to die, how brave we will be and how others will be affected by our deaths; and we use the knowledge of our shared mortality to try and persuade others to love us better now.

Actual crisis

The news that we are actually facing a life-threatening situation, or the experience of accompanying others who are in fact on their deathbeds, both feel quite different from our fantasies entertained while no actual crisis exists. New insights and reflections arise. An austere kind of blessing can become available at this point of crisis, which we cannot find elsewhere.

Immediate grief

The bereaved find themselves suddenly in a state that afflicts the living survivors in a complex and visceral way, which has to be worked through over time as they deal with the irreversible fact of their loved one's death. They are often surprised to find that grief consists of a whole range of emotions that wash over them unpredictably. These can include a feeling of numbness or insubstantiality, sadness, boredom, deep anger, guilt and physical pain. They may wish to talk endlessly of the dead, and may have convincing fantasies or dreams that the person has come back to life. There are immediate administrative and ritual tasks to be accomplished, and a whole new range of people who accompany them at this time.

Remembering and celebrating

Initially the memories of those who have died are around the actual death, but gradually the earlier memories of a fully lived life can emerge, and a rounded, poignant sense of the individual who is remembered. In thinking about actual people who have lived and died on this earth, whether we knew them personally or not, it becomes easier to access a sense of wholeness and meaning to the shape of human existence, and celebrate our place in the unending sequence of living and dying.

Hope

Christians have the hope and promise of a life with God that embraces us beyond death as well as during this life on earth. However, we have very little further information about this, and Christians are not exempt from fears, fantasies and speculation about our own deaths, or from the normal sequence of grief reactions that afflict bereaved human beings generally. The hope that we hold is based on the conviction that God in Christ shared our human lives up to and including the experience of death, and yet was raised in power on the third day. Thus we have the assurance that the sting of death and the victory of the grave (however powerful from an earthly perspective) have been overcome. The God who brought us to birth and has supported us through the joys and vicissitudes of life will also embrace us in death. This conviction may enable us to surrender ourselves to the one who holds our whole story – our unremembered beginning and our unforeseeable end – and will always defend and befriend us:

Before the beginning thou hast foreknown the end,
Before the birthday the death-bed was seen of thee:
Cleanse what I cannot cleanse, mend what I cannot mend,
O Lord, All-Merciful, be merciful to me.

While the end is drawing near I know not mine end;
Birth I recall not, my death I cannot foresee:
O God, arise to defend, arise to befriend,
O Lord All-Merciful, be merciful to me.

Christina Rossetti

ORDINARY MORTALITY

Fern Hill

Now as I was young and easy under the apple boughs
About the lilting house and happy as the grass was green,
   The night above the dingle starry,
    Time let me hail and climb
   Golden in the heydays of his eyes,
And honoured among wagons I was prince of the apple towns
And once below a time I lordly had the trees and leaves
   Trail with daisies and barley
  Down the rivers of the windfall light.

And as I was green and carefree, famous among the barns
About the happy yard and singing as the farm was home,
   In the sun that is young once only,
    Time let me play and be
   Golden in the mercy of his means,
And green and golden I was huntsman and herdsman, the calves
Sang to my horn, the foxes on the hills barked clear and cold,
   And the sabbath rang slowly
  In the pebbles of the holy streams.

All the sun long it was running, it was lovely, the hay
Fields high as the house, the tunes from the chimneys, it was air
   And playing, lovely and watery
    And fire green as grass.
   And nightly under the simple stars
As I rode to sleep the owls were bearing the farm away,
All the moon long I heard, blessed among stables, the nightjars
   Flying with the ricks, and the horses
    Flashing into the dark.

And then to awake, and the farm, like a wanderer white
With the dew, come back, the cock on his shoulder: it was all
   Shining, it was Adam and maiden,
    The sky gathered again
   And the sun grew round that very day,
So it must have been after the birth of the simple light
In the first, spinning place, the spellbound horses walking warm
   Out of the whinnying green stable
    On to the fields of praise.

And honoured among foxes and pheasants by the gay house
Under the new made clouds and happy as the heart was long,
  In the sun born over and over,
    I ran my heedless ways,
  My wishes raced through the house high hay,
And nothing I cared, at my sky blue trades, that time allows
In all his tuneful turning so few and such morning songs
  Before the children green and golden
    Follow him out of grace,

Nothing I cared, in the lamb white days, that time would take me
Up to the swallow thronged loft by the shadow of my hand,
  In the moon that is always rising,
    Nor that riding to sleep
  I should hear him fly with the high fields
And wake to the farm forever fled from the childless land.
Oh as I was young and easy in the mercy of his means,
    Time held me green and dying
  Though I sang in my chains like the sea.

Dylan Thomas

It may seem strange to begin a book about dying with a poem that is full of the exuberance of life, specifically the energetic life and play of a young child. But perhaps the necessary task of accepting our ordinary human mortality is best approached not through fear or despair, but everyday joy.

Dylan Thomas' poetry almost demands to be read out loud. When we do this, some of the liberties he takes with words (he has been described as drunk with language) begin to make sense: the strange adjectives, the grammar that doesn't quite resolve itself, the echoes of familiar phrases that have been adapted for new use. In 'Fern Hill', this quirky language seems brilliantly applied, since it is almost as if a young child is experimenting with language, as with everything else in his play-world, lord of all he surveys.

Thomas was brought up in Swansea, but his city life was balanced with summers spent with his aunt at the farm in Carmarthenshire where the poem is set. This may explain why the boy's rural experience is recalled as everlasting summer and freedom to play. It is as if there are no chills or shadows in this Edenic place, where the skies are clear and all of creation, animals, fruits and harvest seem to be part of the child's dominion of imaginative play. Yet the poem is saved from cloying nostalgia precisely because of the reader's awareness that childhood passes, and because the echoes of Eden themselves suggest what happened there in the biblical account: the fall from innocence, the beginning of shame, the entry of painfully hard work, the certainty of death (Genesis 3).

The poet captures the perspective of childhood in a variety of ways, which remind us that this is not how adults see the world. There is a repeated metaphor of the hayfields which are as 'high as the house', for a child running through the grown crop can hardly see the house beside it, while an adult would see the whole landscape. Various phrases recur that are redolent of the clichés of children's books, but subtly altered. Instead of 'happy as the day was long' we have 'happy as the grass was green', 'singing as the farm was home', 'happy as the heart was long'. For a period of time, it is as if these things were true; the child was temporarily wholeheartedly located in the happy narratives that adults recount to children – the hero of his own triumphant stories.

The narrator is seemingly re-entering his own childhood play, with its exact combination of a glorious delight in the ordinary features of the natural world, and a sense of personal dominion untrammelled by adult knowledge, desires or responsibilities. He is 'prince of the apple towns', he 'lordly' wreathes the trees with trails of daisy chains, he imagines himself a hunter, or a magnificent rider, 'honoured among wagons'. He feels like Adam, the first created man, present at the birth of creation's light, orchestrating worship of God as he lets out the whinnying horses 'On to the fields of praise'. Night and day celebrate with him 'All the sun long' and 'All the moon long'.

But there is another strand that underlies this exuberance. The metaphor of greenness pervades the poem, sometimes intermingled with gold – again that sense of perpetual sunshine so often recalled by children, and not by their accompanying adults. In Thomas' work, greenness represents the life-force, the fuse of youthfulness, energy and vitality that brings growth and fertility. Yet 'green' also conveys the suggestion of naivety, oblivious to the cynicism, pain, disappointment, guilt and failure (including the failure to be a hero) that will come with adulthood.

And then there is the figure of time itself, that (in spite of the child's sense of his own dominion) is actually in control throughout the poem. It begins by letting the child 'play and be/ Golden', but moves on remorselessly to the point where childhood is imperceptibly lost, as the 'children green and golden/ Follow him out of grace'. At one level there is a gentleness implied by the child's right to this time of blissful and careless unawareness, 'young and easy in the mercy of his means'; but at another we are reminded how we are permitted only 'so few and such morning songs' in this life.

But this is the deal. From the time we are born we are also on the way to our deaths. Even as a child 'Time held me green and dying' (notice the precise choice of that word 'held', which can imply both comfort and bondage). But this ordinary mortality, poignant and limited as it is, is also glorious and can be accepted and inhabited with childlike joy. We share the bonds of creation, but we too can choose to sing in our 'chains like the sea'.

In the Fields

Lord, when I look at lovely things which pass,
  Under old trees the shadows of young leaves
Dancing to please the wind along the grass,
  Or the gold stillness of the August sun on the August sheaves;
Can I believe there is a heavenlier world than this?
  And if there is
Will the strange heart of any everlasting thing
  Bring me these dreams that take my breath away?
They come at evening with the home-flying rooks and the scent of hay,
  Over the fields. They come in Spring.

Charlotte Mew

It is not, of course, only human childhood that passes quickly. The conditions of change – new growth, maturity, ripeness, ageing and death – are all around us in the natural world and the passing of the seasons. No moment of beauty is static or possible to capture; there is only a brief opportunity to gaze at 'lovely things which pass'.

It is hard to write in an original way about the beauties of nature, and the poet has chosen a few select details to focus on. Concentrating on the wind in the trees, she has, instead of looking upwards, directed our gaze downwards to the shadows of the leaves, which appear to be flickering and dancing across the grass. With very few words she highlights the temporary and yet recurring nature of the scene's beauty (the trees are old, the leaves are new; this will happen repeatedly). And she implies a sort of loving playfulness between the elements of the scene by personifying them. It is as if the leaves are 'Dancing to please' the wind-blown grass beneath them. The next line chooses another detail of the changing face of the land-scape: 'the gold stillness of the August sun on the August sheaves'. Here the wind has dropped; the harvest is cut; the moment of ripe-ness has been achieved and it almost seems as if time itself has stopped in the golden heat. The repetition of the word 'August' in one short line implies this – and yet, of course, it also reminds us that September and the cool rains will come. It is lovely, but it is not for ever.

This brief poem's central question comes next: 'Can I believe there is a heavenlier world than this?' After the pictures just painted, this could be simply an expression of delight in the natural landscape. But it also exposes the problems for those of us who want to believe there is a heaven. How on earth can we envisage loveliness more detailed and intense than the glory this life is capable of unfolding to us? And how shall we ever be able to bear leaving it behind, as we must one day do? Those who have been privileged to accompany someone who has faced their death with awareness and clarity will recognize that this is a particular kind of grief that the dying do experience. The sight, sounds and scents of the natural world become more tender and important to them, even if the scope for experiencing these is limited to a glimpse of the weather through a bedroom window or the nearness of a loved animal or a vase of flowers. It is hard to leave this world that connects our bodies and our senses to whatever grasp we have of what beauty is.

The poem goes on to try and explore the idea of a 'heavenlier world'. For it is as if her response to the natural world awakes more mysterious longings – 'dreams that take my breath away'. It does not seem possible to her that 'the strange heart of any everlasting thing' can compete with the ever-changing fields in stirring her soul. Earthliness, temporary beauty, evanescence itself feel necessary to experience what is deepest in her. Is the concept of what is 'everlasting' in fact as moving to the human soul as are the actual 'lovely things which pass'?

For some of us, these may be enough – or, at least, all that we can believe there is – and perhaps this is what the poet means. And yet I notice that the poem is almost in the form of a prayer; it starts with the invocation 'Lord'. It is an open question what we can believe about a world beyond this infinitely precarious, infinitely precious one that we know.

Plums

When their time comes they fall
without wind, without rain.
They seep through the trees' muslin
in a slow fermentation.

Daily the low sun warms them
in a late love that is sweeter
than summer. In bed at night
we hear heartbeat of fruitfall.

The secretive slugs crawl home
to the burst honeys, are found
in the morning mouth on mouth,
inseparable.

We spread patchwork counterpanes
for a clean catch. Baskets fill,
never before such harvest,
such a hunters' moon burning

the hawthorns, drunk on syrups
that are richer by night
when spiders pitch
tents in the wet grass.

This morning the red sun
is opening like a rose
on our white wall, prints there
the fishbone shadow of a fern.

The early blackbirds fly
guilty from a dawn haul
of fallen fruit. We too
breakfast on sweetnesses.

Soon plum trees will be bone,
grown delicate with frost's
formalities. Their black
angles will tear the snow.

Gillian Clarke

9

It does not seem possible for us to contemplate the stages of life, maturity and death within the natural world without finding there a powerful metaphor for our own ageing and mortality. This richly observed poem by Gillian Clarke about the ripening of the harvest of plums does not stray into any explicit speculation about human dying, still less about anything that may lie beyond death. But somehow human experience is woven into the whole description, attentive as it is to the essential 'plumminess' of these ripening and then fermenting plums, desired and devoured by so many in creation, including ourselves. I wonder as I read it whether there is an implied tribute to a famous, very short, intense poem by Wallace Stevens about ripe plums left in the fridge overnight, eaten without permission by the poet. Plums seem to stand for something about the intoxicating but transient sweetness of life itself.

The connection to human mortality is suggested by the very first line: 'When their time comes they fall'. The phrase about time is commonly applied to our own expectations of mortality, and there is something quite soothing about the tone here. There is no sense of struggle or violence about ripening or falling to the ground; unbattered by rough weather, the plums 'seep' from the trees as gently as if they were passing through a muslin cloth (something used to sieve out everything but the juices, when making jelly from fruit). Could our own experience of dying in any way be like this gentle subsidence into 'a slow fermentation'?

The second stanza beautifully captures the distinctive autumn 'low sun', which nevertheless retains significant heat. The resonances are sensual, even erotic. It warms the plums 'in a late love that is sweeter/ than summer' (fallen fruit is indeed soft and warm to the touch). There are hints that human lives also can yield experiences of love in later life that may rival or exceed the loves of youth. And indeed we immediately move to the night-time bedroom where 'we hear heartbeat of fruitfall'. 'Heartbeat' is exactly right to evoke the soft, almost imperceptible thump of soft fruit on the ground, perhaps so frequent that it seems regular as a pulse. And, of course, it brings intimately close the falling of the fruit and the embrace of the sleepy couple. The erotic theme continues in an extraordinary third stanza, which contrives to represent even the slugs who are attracted to the fruit as sexy beasts – 'secretive', desiring the 'burst honeys', discovered 'mouth on mouth' the next morning.

The human agents in the narrative take action to protect the windfalls from bruising, and from too much attention from the slugs in the grass. The traditional technique is to lay old, patched bed linen under the trees to achieve 'a clean catch'; the pale sheets or counterpanes make the plums show up well, and provide a simple way to gather the fruit. Anyone who has a mature plum tree knows that there can be staggering weight of fruit, which falls quickly and creates a glut. Here the poet again paints a picture of richness and excess in an autumn world 'drunk on syrups': the distinctively bright autumn moon; the scarlet hedgerow berries; the dew-sodden spiders' webs. The time of ripening feels like completion, fullness and glory.

This tone continues as the early morning sun is described, or at least its reflected rose-red light on the bedroom wall. But then a note of death creeps in: the shadow of the fern that is 'printed' there is reminiscent of a fishbone. The analogy is precise, conveying the delicate, dissected shape of the fern's complicated leaf pattern. But it hints at the skeletal. The next stanza moves from the passion of the slugs to the guilt of the blackbirds; the suggestion is no longer about an intimate embrace but a dawn raid. And the humans are implicated. 'We too/ breakfast on sweetnesses' – the plural word implies the pleasures of excess.

Finally the poem acknowledges how transient is the enjoyment of this intense harvest. The trees will not just be bare, they will be 'bone'. Like the fern-print made by the reddening sun, they will again become 'delicate with frost's/ formalities'. There is a sense of polite distancing here, in contrast with the unashamed, seductive cornucopia when the fruit was ready for eating. And then the tone is not just reserved, it is ominous. The poem envisages the shape of the bare branches against the winter landscape as violent: 'their black/ angles will tear the snow'. Suddenly there is the painful reality of loss, grief, death. This will be true for the human lovers also, when their winter of separation arrives. Yet this last sentence is the only sharp moment in the poem. Overall, the mood is about rejoicing in ripeness, and revelling in sweetnesses in that short moment when they are offered to us to taste.

The Burning of the Leaves

(Section 1)

Now is the time for the burning of the leaves.
They go to the fire; the nostril pricks with smoke
Wandering slowly into a weeping mist.
Brittle and blotched, ragged and rotten sheaves!
A flame seizes the smouldering ruin and bites
On stubborn stalks that crackle as they resist.

The last hollyhock's fallen tower is dust;
All the spices of June are a bitter reek,
All the extravagant riches spent and mean.
All burns! The reddest rose is a ghost;
Sparks whirl up, to expire in the mist: the wild
Fingers of fire are making corruption clean.

Now is the time for stripping the spirit bare,
Time for the burning of days ended and done,
Idle solace of things that have gone before:
Rootless hopes and fruitless desire are there;
Let them go to the fire, with never a look behind.
The world that was ours is a world that is ours no more.

They will come again, the leaf and the flower, to arise
From squalor of rottenness into the old splendour,
And magical scents to a wondering memory bring;
The same glory, to shine upon different eyes.
Earth cares for her own ruins, naught for ours.
Nothing is certain, only the certain spring.

Laurence Binyon

This poem, which is the first section of a much longer poem by Laurence Binyon, is also about autumn, but its tone is very different from the preceding text by Gillian Clarke. Rather than luxuriating in the richness of the year's harvest, its setting is that rather later part of the year where everything has died back and it is time in the garden to clear up plant debris and put everything on a bonfire. Anyone who has a garden will recognize the accuracy of the scene: the showers of dust and dry seeds from the herbaceous plants as they are cut down; the pungent and rotten smells from overblown flower heads that were fragrant in summer; the crackling of the bonfire as dry stalks blaze; the smoke that catches eyes and nose and makes you weep as you tend the fire.

But, of course, this poem is not just about the fun involved in having a great bonfire. Binyon is perhaps best known as one of the war poets of the First World War, and his ode 'For the Fallen' is regularly used at Remembrance Day services still ('They shall not grow old, as we that are left grow old'). Born in 1869, Binyon was too old to fight in the Great War, though he did volunteer as a medical orderly. 'The Burning of the Leaves' was written in 1942, in the middle of yet another global conflict, and the poem, set in Remembrance tide, at the back end of autumn, evokes some of the exhaustion, bitterness and even despair that must have been in the air, when no one knew when this war would end or what its outcome would be.

The poem works at two levels simultaneously. The very first line, while being truthful about the seasons of the gardening year – 'Now is the time for the burning of the leaves' – implies also quite other things that need to be relinquished. It is not stated what these are, but they could be personal regrets or pointless dreams (later, the narrator mentions 'Rootless hopes and fruitless desire'), or destructive ideologies that have yet again convulsed the world, or just, in age, the need to finally let go of memories or aspects of the past that no longer have any capacity to nourish the soul. This is the writing of someone who has lived through anguished, turbulent and austere times, and himself is facing the end of his life (he died in 1943). There is a satisfaction in seeing dead things being devoured by fire, as the poem highlights the ugliness of what must be destroyed: 'Brittle and blotched, ragged and rotten sheaves!' The alliteration conveys a sense of contempt, and seems to approve the viciousness of the fire, which 'bites' old, resistant stalks that are personified as 'stubborn', like defeated enemies.

The image of the dead stalk of hollyhock as a 'fallen tower' is brilliant, since the flower does reach an astonishing and commanding height, and sprays seeds as its spires are taken down. But the image, like its companion 'the smouldering ruin' in the first stanza, calls forth the contemporary scenes that would have been only too familiar: the actual towers and spires that were bombed and shelled to the ground in both wars, and the fires that followed. Again, there is some savage delight in the power of 'wild/ Fingers of fire' to devour the rubbish and cleanse corruption. It should be noted that at this time in the war, the horror of the death camps in Europe and the genocidal use of gas and fire had not been exposed to the world.

For the narrator now reaches the heart of the poem's imagery. Echoing the start of the first line, 'Now is the time for stripping the spirit bare', it is a call to extinguish nostalgia about times past. The sibilant consonants continue, hissing at the reader: 'solace', 'Rootless', 'fruitless'; this must have been a hard message to receive from a poet in this era. No family had been untouched by grief and loss in the Great War, and afterwards there were waves of unresolved sadness and desire to make contact with the dead. Now there was yet more loss of life, relationships and homes, yet the poem instructs 'Let them go to the fire . . . The world that was ours is a world that is ours no more.' In one sense, this is true for everyone who reaches an advanced age and has to face that the energy and agency that was theirs in youth has passed on, and this hard fact has to be accepted. But there seems to be a wider sense here of a world where a whole way of life has been lost and there will be a need to rebuild from the ground upwards.

The final stanza of this section returns to the natural world, the promise of renewal inherent in the reliability of the seasons and the confident expectation that death and decay will be replaced with new vigour and splendour. But the implication is that this natural cycle, so potent as an image for human life, actually happens quite independently of human hopes – 'Earth cares for her own ruins, naught for ours.' Even the beauties that will spring again will 'shine upon different eyes'. For humans who face their own mortality, 'Nothing is certain' because the 'certain spring' may not be seen by them.

Fidele's Dirge

Fear no more the heat o' th' sun
   Nor the furious winter's rages;
Thou thy worldly task hast done,
   Home art gone, and ta'en thy wages.
Golden lads and girls all must,
As chimney-sweepers, come to dust.

Fear no more the frown o' th' great;
   Thou art past the tyrant's stroke.
Care no more to clothe and eat;
   To thee the reed is as the oak.
The sceptre, learning, physic, must
All follow this and come to dust.

Fear no more the lightning flash,
   Nor th' all-dreaded thunder-stone;
Fear not slander, censure rash;
   Thou hast finish'd joy and moan.
All lovers young, all lovers must
Consign to thee and come to dust.

No exorciser harm thee!
Nor no witchcraft charm thee!
Ghost unlaid forbear thee!
Nothing ill come near thee!
Quiet consummation have,
And renowned be thy grave!

William Shakespeare

Like a number of Shakespeare's songs, this dirge, which appears in *Cymbeline*, has a gentle poignancy about the inevitability of death that must come to us all. It has the feel of a traditional bittersweet folk song, with the concluding stanza being a kind of spell of protection for the repose of the spirit of the departed. Set to music many times, it is sometimes used at funeral services as a fitting comment about someone who has lived a long life and has achieved a good deal, sometimes in the face of difficulties and opposition.

However, the way the song functions in the play is rather different from the way it reads when lifted out of that context. It is sung antiphonally by two brothers, Guiderius and Arviragus, who will later turn out to be long-lost princes. They are mourning the beautiful youth Fidele, who is actually their young sister Imogen in disguise – and she turns out shortly afterwards to be not really dead. So the beauty of the song and the sense of loss expressed is doing more to convey the instinctive connection these characters have with each other than it is in lamenting human mortality. And yet the song has an independent power to move us.

Although it is a funeral song, there is a calm and reassuring tone to this poem, which is as if addressed to the person who has just died, comforting him or her that the tribulations of this hard life are over, and it is time to settle into eternal rest. Usually, of course, it is death itself that strikes fear into the human heart, rather than the incidental problems of managing our lives in this world. So for the singer or hearer of this song, the injunction to 'Fear no more', apparently about the hardship of life, functions to make us feel calmer about the reality that death comes to us all. It represents death as a release from the kind of anxieties that may grip us daily: managing an ageing and vulnerable body that copes with both heat and cold not as well as it used to; worrying about what we have achieved in this life. Death is a 'Home' that can be reached, and the 'wages' – whether just the completion of our tasks or the just deserts we may receive in the next life – will be fairly sorted.

The mention of 'Golden lads and girls' (highly appropriate to a dirge for 'Fidele', who is both a lad and a girl) speaks of how even youth is headed towards the dust, like every human being. The biblical story in Genesis tells how the first human being was created by God from the dust of the earth, and after the fall from grace and expulsion from Eden is told: 'you are dust, and to dust you shall return' (Genesis 3.19) – a phrase uttered over every member of the congregation each year on Ash Wednesday, and recalled, of course, in the funeral service when the body is committed to the ground. In being made of dust and returning to dust, there is an equivalence between all human beings, whether 'golden' with youth or wealth, or the meanest chimney-sweeper, whose very trade entails being coated every day with dust already. But there may be another delightful reference here. In Warwickshire, the dandelions used to be referred to as 'chimney-sweepers' because the flower head is in the exact shape of a chimney-sweeper's brush. And they all turn from bright golden flowers to a soft puffball seed head that can be blown away like dust.

The next stanza widens the scope of what is transient. The dead person need fear no more the capricious earthly powers that could threaten their prosperity in life, or even their life itself. Shakespeare's world was one where the mass of little people had to eke out a living in service to 'th' great' – the small proportion of wealthy landed gentry who employed servants, took rents from those who worked their land, and sponsored the arts, including the theatre. Kings and queens had almost uncontrolled power – the word 'tyrant' is no metaphor, and life around the royal court was fraught with the danger of losing favour. The song echoes the words of Jesus in Luke's Gospel against anxiety: 'do not be anxious about your life, what you shall eat, nor about your body, what you shall put on' (Luke 12.22). And then it makes clear that not only individual human life but all human culture (royal power, academic knowledge, medicine) is headed for oblivion. We are in the realm of the biblical Ecclesiastes, proclaiming the emptiness of all human endeavour: 'Vanity of vanities, says the Preacher, vanity of vanities! All is vanity' (Ecclesiastes 1.2).

The third stanza combines the terrors of the natural world with those of human society. One thinks of the violent thunderstorm in Lear, which exposes his ordinary human vulnerability while mirroring the chaos in his own mind and in the state, which he has left divided by handing over power to his wolfish daughters. The verse ends with death's conquest over even love itself, and here the song is more pessimistic than the Bible. Apparently, love is not as 'strong as death' (Song of Songs 8.6).

It is interesting, given how universally gloomy is the song's theme, that it comes over as essentially comforting. I think the repeated 'Fear no more' has a lot to do with this. It makes the reader or hearer believe that, in spite of everything, there is someone soothing present who is settling the dead into their rest and surrounding them with the magic protection of an incantatory spell of protection. This is the burden of the last stanza. If there are still powers that can disturb the peacefulness of the grave, we will encircle our beloved dead with the power of our blessing.

Ah, God, I may not hate

Ah, God, I may not hate
Myself, who am your thought, who made
Earthworm and spider, gave
Being to the burying-beetle and the maggot,
Beak and talon and teeth, hunger to all creatures
Made to be your begetters and destroyers.
I who am living you from the numberless dead have raised
From the deathless dust of the grave
Dust of gleaming wings born on the wind, seed
In the womb of the wind, borne
In cloud and tempest over the world
On tide and current made and unmade,
I am what you will, what you have willed
Life after life, maggot and spider, seed and harvest,
   chromosome, flame.

Kathleen Raine

Many of the poems in this section have reflected on human life in the context of the natural world, or used the cyclical processes of the natural world to stand for the hopes and fears that humans experience in the face of death. This one, in a rather startling and not very comfortable way, has the poem's narrator explicitly positioning herself as totally at one with the physical processes not only of life and death but of predation and decay.

Where Laurence Binyon's poem has at its centre a bonfire that destroys what is decayed, Kathleen Raine recognizes the part played by the creatures that feast on rottenness, including corpses, in creating the composted soil, and the seed-carrying winds that give birth to new generations of life across the world. The poem is arresting, because usually the contemplation of death has given rise to a sense of horror about being eaten by worms. It is much more consoling to focus on the more conventionally pleasing aspects of the natural world, such as the cycle of the seasons among plant life, with the changing beauties of lushness and austerity as they grow, shoot, flower, fruit and shrivel. Comparing ourselves to burying beetles and maggots (in whose direction we are headed) is certainly a lot less soothing. Perhaps the poet's context in rural Northumberland, with its daily exposure to the processes of life and death, gave her an unflinching realism not always shared by city-dwellers.

Interestingly, the poem is framed as a prayer. It is not a bleak and nihilistic picture that is painted, but an extraordinary sort of celebration of a complex ecosystem, which has been willed by the mind of God. Perhaps anticipating a sort of revulsion in the reader to what she is going to say, it starts with a denial of self-hatred – perhaps implying a tendency to dislike the body and the reality of its ageing. With the powerful line break (we have to pause slightly between 'hate' and 'Myself'), the poet gives us what is almost a credal statement about the significance of human identity in the heart of God: 'Myself, who am your thought'. And yet without pausing for breath, the poem makes our lives equivalent with that of 'Earthworm and spider', and then immediately proceeds to mention creatures we seldom want to think about, namely those that feed on and break down the tissues of corpses. The narrator does not list the diversity of predators that exist in creation, but suggests them by mentioning only some of the tools of aggression built into their bodies: 'Beak and talon and teeth'. I think there is an echo of Tennyson's 'Nature, red in tooth and claw' here (itself part of his massive meditation on mortality, *In Memoriam*). She asserts that God wills this, giving 'hunger to all creatures'.

So the poem addresses the reality of how decay and predation are part of how the created world works. Begetting and new life are predicated on the destruction or the reuse of what has lived before. For all the biblical tradition about being created from the dust of the earth, it is not common for human beings to identify ourselves so directly with the lowliest scavengers and composting creatures. But the poem emphasizes this insight, through the slightly archaic and formal word order in the line that is right at its centre: 'I who am living you from the numberless dead have raised'.

The poet has placed the self-assertive phrase 'I who am living' in a prominent position at the start of the line, but then makes it function as the object of the verb, so it means, 'You have raised me from the numberless dead'. The powerful language about raising the dead is not accidental. She is referring to the reality in which the atoms of our body are made up of matter that has belonged elsewhere in the universe first, but presenting this as if it were a biblical miracle about the raising of the dead. It is as if we arise into our lives directly from the 'deathless dust of the grave'.

The continuing list becomes like a psalm of praise to the minutiae of how creation is 'made and unmade', where tiny, detailed creatures or winged seeds are carried by forces of weather across seas and continents to perpetuate life elsewhere. It is a mystery redolent of some of the poetry of the book of Job, who classically challenges God on the subject of death and suffering. He is answered by a paean about the beauty, terror and complexity of the created world, which is willed by God but not subject to individual human understanding (Job 38).

The poem is deeply at odds with our usual focus on the importance of individuals and our separate souls, instead locating our bodies firmly within the laws of physical life even to its lowest levels, and humbly declaring simply, 'I am what you will, what you have willed/ Life after life'. Interestingly, however, after reiterating the maggot and spider, and referring to traditional harvest imagery, the poet allows a single image that may take us beyond the dying body. We are not just 'chromosome' but 'flame'. In the whole poem there are only two sentences; it goes on and on, just as does the sequence of 'life after life' that it conveys.

A Hindu to His Body

Dear pursuing presence,
dear body: you brought me
curled in womb and memory.

Gave me fingers to clutch
at grace, at malice; and ruffle
someone else's hair; to fold a man's
shadow back on his world;
to hold in the dark of the eye
through a winter and a fear
the poise, the shape of a breast;
a pear's silence, in the calyx
and the noise of a childish fist.

You brought me: do not leave me
behind. When you leave all else,
my garrulous face, my unkissed
alien mind, when you muffle
and put away my pulse

to rise in the sap of trees
let me go with you and feel the weight
of honey-hives in my branching
and the burlap weave of weaver-birds
in my hair.

A. K. Ramanujan

In contrast with the rather austere tone of Kathleen Raine's poem, this one by A. K. Ramanujan, which also explores the way our mortality locates us within the wider creation, evokes a real tenderness in its meditation on the body. The title, 'A Hindu to His Body', inevitably references the classic Hindu belief in the reincarnation of the soul, in which each body that is lived in is discarded when the soul migrates to its next incarnation. But the poem's take on this doctrine is distinctive; there is no sense that only the soul, the 'me' who is in dialogue with the body, has importance. Rather, the growing and then gradually ageing body is addressed with affection and indeed deep need. It is his own body, and not a divinity, that the narrator is addressing.

The 'me' who is the voice of the poem expresses nothing but love for his body, in contrast with cultures that despise the body or seek only to subjugate it in the interests of the eternal soul. It is almost as if the body can be thought of as like a divine or angelic being who provides comfort to humanity. 'Dear pursuing presence,/ dear body' is a beautifully expressed image of the body as an attendant to the mind or soul, but a strong and maternal one. Everything about the narrator's being has been carried to him via the body itself; even his memory is contained in the body. It is the body that has enabled engagement with the world, from earliest infancy onwards.

The second stanza suggests, through the infant's touch and sight, some of the crucial experiences of intimacy (but also evil and fear) that will shape the grown man's understanding of what he will face during his bodily life. The juxtaposition of 'fingers to clutch' with the contrasting 'at grace, at malice' illustrates how the tiniest infant is introduced to the range of what the world offers. There seems to be a simultaneous blend of infant and grown-up perceptions in this stanza. To 'ruffle/ someone else's hair' might denote an unconscious grasping of its mother's hair by a breastfeeding child, but also evokes the deliberate affectionate gesture a man might make to someone he loves. I do not really know what folding 'a man's/ shadow back on his world' means; perhaps it is about the power of the newborn infant to completely reorder his father's sense of identity. The gaze of the infant towards the all-crucial breast, with its distinctive 'poise' and 'shape' and power to dispel fear, also seems to foreshadow the speaker's grown-up attraction, even devotion, to the female body with its awesome ability to evoke the attachments and reassurance of the time before speech.

The third stanza is like a plea to a beloved mother or a lover not to be deserted by the body that brought the person into being. This poem was written in midlife; there is the sense of the inevitability of the body's demise and departure. But it is an interesting reversal, as we normally think of the soul or spirit as leaving the body. Here the 'voice' of the poem is identified with the busy and disembodied mind, sometimes uneasily linked to the body (as in the extraordinary phrase 'my garrulous face' – the reader can immediately imagine the needy gaze of the over-talkative small boy or academic young man), sometimes painfully disconnected from it ('my unkissed/ alien mind'). And then the narrator imagines his death as something that his own body seems to be in charge of, as if the pulsing body itself has command over when a pulse will cease and be muffled. How can 'my pulse' be other than my body's pulse?

So the poem ends with the desire not to migrate to a bodiless state or begin life in a new body, but to 'go with you' into the wider created world beyond that of humanity. Here the contribution made by the composting of the body towards new life is uplifting and positive. The narrator desires to 'rise in the sap of trees' with his body and, as if he is at one with the tree, to feel the weight of the nests of other creatures – honeybees and weaver-birds 'in my hair'. He is tactile to the end, celebrating the body in all its phases and reluctant to be separated from it.

The Flower

How fresh, O Lord, how sweet and clean
Are thy returns! E'en as the flowers in Spring,
   To which, besides their own demesne,
The late-past frosts tributes of pleasure bring;
     Grief melts away
     Like snow in May,
As if there were no such cold thing.

Who would have thought my shrivelled heart
Could have recovered greenness? It was gone
   Quite under ground; as flowers depart
To see their mother-root, when they have blown,
     Where they together
     All the hard weather,
Dead to the world, keep house unknown.

These are thy wonders, Lord of power,
Killing and quickening, bringing down to Hell
   And up to Heaven in an hour;
Making a chiming of a passing-bell.
     We say amiss
     This or that is;
Thy word is all, if we could spell.

O that I once past changing were,
Fast in thy Paradise, where no flower can wither;
   Many a spring I shoot up fair,
Offering at Heaven, growing and groaning thither;
     Nor doth my flower
     Want a spring-shower,
My sins and I joining together.

But while I grow in a straight line,
Still upwards bent, as if Heaven were mine own,
   Thy anger comes, and I decline:
What frost to that? what pole is not the zone
     Where all things burn,
     When thou dost turn,
And the least frown of thine is shown?

The Flower

And now in age I bud again,
After so many deaths I live and write;
  I once more smell the dew and rain,
And relish versing: O, my only Light,
    It cannot be
    That I am he
On whom thy tempests fell at night.

These are thy wonders, Lord of love,
To make us see we are but flowers that glide;
  Which when we once can find and prove,
Thou hast a garden for us where to bide;
    Who would be more,
    Swelling through store,
Forfeit their Paradise by their pride.

George Herbert

This whole poem is based on a very traditional observation, namely that the life of human beings is as transient as that of a flower, springing up, withering, dying and becoming rubbish for the bonfire. The analogy recalls the meditation in the psalms on this theme (for example, Psalm 90.5–6), but also the saying of Jesus, 'Consider the lilies' (Luke 12.27–28).

So it is a well-known image, but Herbert addresses the life cycle of the flower in an arresting way. Speaking as if directly to God, with whom he is in comfortable conversation, he words his opening praise as if he is exclaiming with delight about the first spring flowers, which have a cool beauty that pierces the gloomy end of winter. He is referring to God's 'returns' – a term that seems to bear several levels of meaning: the spring's anniversary (rather in the sense that we wish people 'many happy returns' on their birthday); the sense of blessing, which feels like the turning of God's face towards the speaker; and the gracious and unearned benefits God brings to human beings (as in the sense of returning good for evil, or bringing a return on investment). So initially it is God's blessings that are like the flowers in spring – felt as special precisely because of the hardships that may have preceded them. The first flowers of spring bring comfort out of proportion to their intrinsic beauty because they emerge from the 'late-past frosts'. The frost and cold suddenly lose their power, even in recent memory, just as an unseasonal snowfall fails to last as soon

25

as the sun comes up. Yet we recognize that we are not just speaking about the transition to warmth and life in the natural world. It is human suffering: 'Grief melts away/ Like snow in May,/ As if there were no such cold thing.'

Note how every word is ordinary and single-syllabled, but the short words fall like hammer blows. Of course there is such a cold thing as snow, and grief. We know they will return.

The next stanza moves the flower image swiftly into the suffering human heart of the narrator. In the context of praising newly sprung flowers at the end of winter, the reference to his heart as 'shrivelled' but then recovering 'greenness' is a brilliant evocation of many of the natural processes that have been happening to seeds, bulbs and tubers during the dark and cold. He expands the metaphor to chart what has been happening to plants in the autumn, as the flowers blow over and die, and a plant becomes dormant, withdrawing all its recoverable sap back into the parts of it that remain under the ground and will survive the cold. The language Herbert uses, about a period of what must have been profound depression, is actually rather comforting. The flowers in winter are simply visiting their 'mother-root', where she keeps 'house unknown' deep below the surface. The dark time is not about hopelessness and death; it is about preparing for new life, even when no signs of life are apparent.

The third stanza reflects on God's 'wonders', but the tone has shifted into something less comfortable. The term 'wonder' did not automatically mean something positive in Herbert's time; it could be something remarkable but chilling. And here he highlights how a God of power can arrange for matters of life and death to occur suddenly and regularly – 'Killing and quickening', almost as if the sound of the passing bell (the traditional way of proclaiming that someone has died) has become the ticking of a clock that tells the hours. Things we believe simply *are*, and will never change, do in fact die or pass on without warning. Only the word of God remains unchanging. Everything else – like the evidently transient flower that springs up vigorously – is subject to mortality, however energetic its apparent life and growth.

The next stanza reapplies the image again, this time to the narrator, or at least to his purposes and intentions. At first expressing a longing to be safely in Paradise, that place where the grass will not wither nor the flower fade, the narrator speaks of how he (or the springs of his ambitions) 'shoot up fair' towards heaven, but do so in a way that leaves them fragile and subject to being easily destroyed. He speaks of 'My sins and I joining together'. I think Herbert wants the reader to have in mind the parables of Jesus that speak of seeds that try to grow the word of God, but in the wrong kind of ground, which end up rootless and shrivelled or else choked by weeds (Mark 4.1–18).

The fifth stanza defines the sin more closely as one of pride. It seems that the narrator is doing well in his life before God, and growing strongly heavenwards. But he falls into the belief that his reward is assured, achieved through his own efforts 'as if Heaven were mine own'. And this attracts God's anger. Good intention has been corrupted by the sin of pride, and the plant that stands for the poet is blasted by God's anger – here the destructive power of the burning sun rather than frosts.

And yet the plant of devotion and hope has not died. As can happen with many plants, apparent destruction has given way to new buds. The application of the image has shifted again. Again it focuses on the narrator's own life, but specifically around his ability both to appreciate the natural world and to engage in writing poetry. It is clear that Herbert used his English poetry as an intimate way of relating to God, so 'versing' is deeply bound in with his spiritual journey and his sense of how he stands with God. He speaks about budding again 'in age'. Given that Herbert died before the age of 50, it may well give the contemporary reader pause for thought about how the meaning of ageing has changed. The words 'so many deaths' could refer to his own brushes with serious illness; to the deaths of dear friends; to the collapse of his ambitions to be significant at court; or to the periods of dark depression to which he seems to have been prone, and which may have affected his capacity to write. The observation about smelling 'the dew and rain' again evokes the cool freshness and sweetness of the poem's start. We are made aware of the renewed sharpness of awakened sense impressions, once the grey veil of depression is lifted. There is a sense of being renewed in his whole being, just as the experience of a turbulent and sleepless night can be shed by the gift of a bright morning.

The final stanza returns to the word 'wonders'. Having visited the term in the third verse, and explored the rather fearsome power of God to kill and quicken in rapid succession, he now affirms that the true wonders God brings us are those of love. The gift is that of simple understanding that, with all our self-importance and desire to achieve recognition through our own efforts, 'we are but flowers that glide' – that is, beautiful, created by God, but evanescent. We may bloom gloriously but we do not last, not on this earth. The garden that is for ever is elsewhere; but we can lose our promised place in it by trying to convince ourselves that we are what we are not. So this intimate poem ends on a slight note of warning, reminding us that, like the rest of Herbert's poetry, it is for him a way of undertaking serious self-examination in prayer. His readiness for heaven, and whether or not his pride will get in the way of this, is what is eternally at stake here.

FEARS AND FANTASIES

The Hill

Breathless, we flung us on the windy hill,
  Laughed in the sun, and kissed the lovely grass.
  You said, 'Through glory and ecstasy we pass;
Wind, sun, and earth remain, the birds sing still,
When we are old, are old . . .' 'And when we die
  All's over that is ours; and life burns on
Through other lovers, other lips,' said I,
  'Heart of my heart, our heaven is now, is won!'

'We are Earth's best, that learnt her lesson here.
  Life is our cry. We have kept the faith!' we said;
  'We shall go down with unreluctant tread
Rose-crowned into the darkness!' . . . Proud we were,
And laughed, that had such brave true things to say.
– And then you suddenly cried, and turned away.

Rupert Brook

If the poems in the first section explore the ordinary givens of human mortality, and our connectedness through that reality with the wider creation, those in this section go into the range of fears and fantasies that can surround our attempts to contemplate the idea of our own personal deaths, when the actual prospect is still distant.

This remarkable poem by Rupert Brook, written in 1911 when he was in his early twenties (when he could not have known that, along with so many young men of his generation, he would die before he was 30), has all the energy and idealism of youth. It is written as a sonnet, and uses the discipline and the possibilities of the form to the full. Starting without explanation as to who 'we' are, the reader is suddenly brought (panting) to the summit of a hill. Presumably a young couple have climbed it rather fast and are now exulting in their achievement and in their total delight in each other simultaneously. The sibilant consonants echo the heavy breathing that their vigorous exercise has brought on: 'Breathless', 'kissed', 'grass'. Almost nothing is said about the two speakers in the poem, even that they are lovers; this is only said indirectly, as they kiss not each other but the grass they fling themselves down on. But their physical success in reaching the summit of the hill suggests an intensely physical chemistry between them, and the way they go on to speak of themselves seems to emerge from experiencing the intoxicating heights of passion.

Virtually the whole of the rest of the poem is carried on the dialogue between them. Within the octet, the first eight lines of the poem that in a sonnet traditionally expound the theme, each lover makes a proud declaration. These are not directed to each other as declarations of love (we have the sense that they are past that stage), but are, interestingly, about mortality and the fact that the wonders of nature will remain after their deaths, and that the 'glory and ecstasy' they have experienced will pass on and envelop the senses and passions of 'other lovers, other lips', as life 'burns on' without them. These are themes that could sound gloomy or poignant, but in this poem we have the sense of sheer triumph in the tone of voice. These are young people who are exulting in the conviction that they have indeed tasted the most glorious joys that life offers, and that they are members of a company of lovers throughout time who have known or will know what it means, truly to live before we die. Heaven, insofar as one exists, has been 'won'.

As we move into the sestet, the last six lines, which traditionally include a significant 'turn' in the meaning, the dialogue seems to continue in the same tone, unabated. But it becomes much less easy to know who is speaking; it is almost as if they are making these announcements together. Having satisfied themselves with their total mutual agreement about the heights of their passion, they go further and declare that they are 'Earth's best'. It is a wonderful observation about young love; from the perspective of middle age and beyond we know that this conclusion about the unique quality of one's passion is reached by virtually all young lovers, who commonly pity their elders (who clearly never felt anything similar in their lives). As they egg each other on to further triumphant declarations, they begin to use the language of religion, or of one of the powerful ideological movements of their contemporary age (whether about free love or political revolution): 'Life is our cry. We have kept the faith!' The reader is beginning to wonder whether this increasingly exaggerated rhetoric will be punctured.

And then there is the final spoken statement between them, this time alleging that, given all this achieved glory, they will, when the time comes, face their deaths proudly and fearlessly, going with 'unreluctant tread/ Rose-crowned into the darkness!' The image is extraordinary, uniting opposites within its aspiration towards courage in the face of death. 'Unreluctant' already introduces, through its very denial of it, the distinct possibility of reluctance to leave life. The juxtaposition of the crown of roses and the darkness yokes together evanescent beauty and annihilation. And the reader cannot help being aware of what happened within a few years of the poem's writing, namely that a generation did indeed go off to war with just such an excited and idealistic approach to the idea of dying crowned with glory.

The real turn of the poem emerges in the last two lines. Recalling the laughter of the opening lines, and the pride of the dialogue so far, the narrator sums them up as having had 'such brave true things to say'. It is a tribute to the maturity of the poet that he was able to communicate the arrogance and magnificence of young love while also placing a distance between himself and the lovers. For that word 'true' generates irony for the reader, if not for the lovers. We know that this blithe courage about the thought of dying is not straightforward or sustainable; we know that dying is seldom simply like going rose-crowned into the darkness. That is a beautiful fantasy, but the reality will be other – or, at least, such simple acceptance of death will take a lifetime of struggle to achieve. And in the last line it seems that the 'you' of the poem has been caught up in the realization of the actual abyss they have been dancing across – and it breaks the connection between them: '– And then you suddenly cried, and turned away.'

I am not Sleeping

I don't want any of that
'We're gathered here today
to celebrate his life, not mourn his passing.'
Oh yes you are. Get one thing straight,
You're not here to celebrate
but to mourn until it hurts.

I want wailing and gnashing of teeth.
I want sobs, and I want them uncontrollable.
I want women flinging themselves on the coffin
and I want them inconsolable.

Don't dwell on my past but on your future.
For what you see is what you'll be,
and sooner than you think.
So get weeping. Fill yourselves with dread.
For I am not sleeping. I am dead.

Roger McGough

The tone of this poem could hardly be more different from the previous one. Downbeat and gloomy, it is full of unashamed fantasy about funerals and apparently determinedly drenched in fear and dread of death. But it is actually deceptively self-aware, and when it is read out loud the reaction is immediate laughter as members of the audience recognize their own embarrassing, unspoken hopes that their personal demise will devastate friends, lovers and family (and that somehow they will have the satisfaction of witnessing that reaction).

This informal, conversational poem in fact sits within a well-known tradition of poems about death, namely the ones you find inscribed on some tombstones of the past. Instead of a serious eulogy to the deceased by their grieving relatives, such an inscription is a text designed to be read by the casual passer-by who strolls over to read the epitaph, and finds himself addressed by the dead person whose corpse he is standing beside. It is the last message of the dead to the living, and it invariably points out gloomily that the living person is only headed in the same direction, so it's time to take stock. Often the text is witty, rather than being just a solemn *memento mori*.

The voice of the poem is immediately established as a querulous one, protesting about the kind of clerical downplaying of the sheer tragedy of death, such as one sometimes gets at funerals. The smooth, upbeat words convey rather precisely the annoyingly patronizing tone of the celebrant who has no emotional connection with the dead person and is offering banal comfort about the importance of celebration rather than mourning. The narrator is dismissive, hectoring the assembled funeral-goers about the demeanour that the corpse in the coffin, by contrast, wants to see going on. They are to 'mourn until it hurts'. The reworking of the traditional phrase 'laugh until it hurts' is instructive. It is as if the person who has died thinks it is quite possible that those who have gathered may not actually be in that much pain, and will need to work a bit harder in order to get into the appropriate gloomy feelings and display enough devastation to satisfy him.

The next stanza is a glorious list of intensely childish demands (a petulant series of repeated 'I wants'). Exaggerated and melodramatic grief cannot being overdone, as far as this corpse is concerned, and all the clichés are introduced: the traditional biblical 'wailing and gnashing of teeth', the uncontrollable sobs, women hysterically flinging themselves on the coffin – something one never actually sees except in gothic fiction (and, presumably, male fantasy life). The florid nature of what the narrator demands, of course, betrays his fear that perhaps he is not so important in anyone's life that their reaction to his death will be particularly dramatic, and perhaps that is true of most of us.

The final stanza is back in the territory of the gravestone that reaches out in warning to the living passer-by, and bids him be afraid – very afraid. 'For what you see is what you'll be,/ and sooner than you think.' But the tongue-in-cheek lecturing style ('So get weeping') again undermines any possible seriousness, as does the clunky, overemphatic rhyming of 'dread' with 'dead'. A poem that is apparently about the fear of death actually ends up being rather cheering, because it's impossible not to laugh, and there is something quite comforting about having the embarrassing contents of someone else's anxious fantasies freely exposed for the absurdities they are.

Indeed, we are all in the same boat and will come to die, but it is possible to experience the fellow-feeling that laughter brings when we do something as frightening as imagining our own death.

The Fly

I heard a Fly buzz – when I died –
The Stillness in the Room
Was like a Stillness in the Air –
Between the Heaves of Storm –

The Eyes around – had wrung them dry –
And Breaths were gathering firm
For that last Onset – when the King
Be witnessed – in the Room –

I willed my Keepsakes – Signed away
What portion of me be
Assignable – and then it was
There interposed a Fly –

With Blue – uncertain stumbling Buzz –
Between the light – and me –
And then the Windows failed – and then
I could not see to see –

Emily Dickinson

Emily Dickinson, a nineteenth-century reclusive poet who wrote an enormous number of poems but published almost nothing in her lifetime, seems to have been almost obsessively curious about death, and especially the process of dying and what it might feel like to die.

The openings of her poems are often arresting, even disturbing, and this one is a cracker. It is hard to imagine a poem about death that would be less likely to make it on to a list of texts suitable for a funeral. The first line introduces the startling notion that a person might be able to speak about their own death in the past tense. I suppose, if a heavenly scene were being imagined, something comforting and uplifting might have been expounded, but the scene is firmly set in the context of a contemporary deathbed, and the observation is about a buzzing fly. This seems to have made its presence felt as the person who is the voice of the poem is actually passing away. This focus is potentially either homely (if distracting) or rather sinister, since the advent of a fly around an imminent death is ominous.

We have to imagine a bedroom scene where members of the family are gathered around the bed to hear the final words and wishes of the dying person. This sort of scene would have been very familiar to someone like Emily Dickinson, who lived at a time when most people would have died at home surrounded by their family, and there would have been ample opportunity to consider in some detail, during various vigils at bedsides, what dying must be like for the person involved. And, of course, when someone dies at home all the normal chores of a household continue around the process (including dealing with any troublesome pests such as house flies during a warm summer).

The first stanza takes us back to explore the sense of stillness in the room, which can occur as someone slips deeper and deeper into the state that precedes the moment of death. But the stillness here is not simply about serenity; it is like the threatening stillness at the eye of a storm when wind, noise and turmoil have preceded it, and the same devastating power is waiting to be unleashed again, in another destabilizing pulse. The poet suggests all this with great economy in the expression 'Heaves of Storm –'.

In the second stanza she makes it clear that the preceding part of the 'Storm' has involved much weeping by those witnessing the event. Rather than describe the people in any detail, the narrator reduces them to 'Eyes' and 'Breaths' – both somewhat in the recovery phase after violent sobbing. It is as if everyone is now aware that death must come soon, and everything is focused on noticing the moment when it comes. The image of the King who is to 'Be witnessed – in the Room –' I find ambiguous. Is the 'King' Death himself? Or is there an expectation that the presence of God will somehow be experienced by the gathering? In any case, the witnesses are preparing themselves for something momentous.

The third stanza seems to be about making a final will and testa-ment (which would certainly imply that the dying woman is capable of dictating something intelligible at least). Historically it was trad-itional for someone to dictate their wishes from their deathbed rather than organize something efficient with lawyers beforehand. But this speaker mentions only 'Keepsakes', conventionally the sort of small personal possessions that were the only things a woman might own in her own right. But something more subtle follows: she signs away 'What portion of me be/ Assignable'; there is an implication here that what can be bequeathed is not the most significant portion of what makes up 'me'. That is the part that will be passing through death to what is beyond. (Traditional wills of the time began by commending the soul to Almighty God, the body to its burial, and only then are the possessions assigned to those who survive.) But this is the moment that the poem began with, as 'There interposed a Fly –'. 'Interpose' brilliantly gives a lawyerly weight to something as trivial as an insect, almost as if it has the power to interrupt and alter a matter of life-and-death significance.

The final stanza captures in an extraordinary way the intermittent, wayward, buzzing progress of this increasingly dominant fly. It has often been observed that the dying appear to retain their sense of hearing as the last shred of sensory awareness before life is extinct, and the poem imagines that this wretched insect, going about its own independent business, seeking the light from the window as flies do, becomes essentially the last thing in life to be experienced by the person who is the poem's voice. Of course, the ordinary light from the window could mean much more than that. Not only does the fly literally intrude 'Between the light – and me –', but the implication is that it gets in the way of the dying person's sense that they are headed towards the light (of God or of heaven) as they move towards death. Finally there is the sense that the ordinary light in the room fails (in fact it is the dying person's sight failing) and 'I could not see to see –'.

The Art of Drowning

I wonder how it all got started, this business
about seeing your life flash before your eyes
while you drown, as if panic, or the act of submergence,
could startle time into such compression, crushing
decades in the vice of your desperate, final seconds.

After falling off a steamship or being swept away
in a rush of floodwaters, wouldn't you hope
for a more leisurely review, an invisible hand
turning the pages of an album of photographs –
you up on a pony or blowing out candles in a conic hat.

How about a short animated film, a slide presentation?
Your life expressed in an essay, or in one model paragraph?
Wouldn't any form be better than this sudden flash?
Your whole existence going off in your face
in an eyebrow-singeing explosion of biography –
nothing like the three large volumes you envisioned.

Survivors would have us believe in a brilliance
here, some bolt of truth forking across the water,
an ultimate Light before all the lights go out,
dawning on you with all its megalithic tonnage.
But if something does flash before your eyes
as you go under, it will probably be a fish,

a quick blur of curved silver darting away,
having nothing to do with your life or your death.
The tide will take you, or the lake will accept it all
as you sink toward the weedy disarray of the bottom,
leaving behind what you have already forgotten,
the surface, now overrun with the high travel of clouds.

Billy Collins

Curiosity about the moment of death pervades this poem by Billy
Collins, in particular the commonly held belief that when you drown,
your whole life passes before you in an instant. Collins' technique
is to examine the tradition in forensic detail, not only exposing the
apparent absurdity of the proposition but also opening up a series

of rueful ruminations on what we may or may not have achieved in our lives, and whether or how these will be celebrated in anyone's memory.

The poem's tone is conversational and genial, speculating about what is believed to happen when you drown: 'I wonder how it all got started . . .' There is no examination of what the physical sensations must be, simply this immensely compressed whole-life experience. But the words used do convey distress: 'panic', 'startle', 'crushing', 'vice', 'desperate'. It is as if the crushing together of all your life's memories stands for whatever it means to drown. This is a violent death, achieved in a short space of time, but long enough to be experienced as frightening and painful. The messy realities of dying this way are not really explored any further, whether or not there actually is a compressed sense of vivid life memories somewhere in the experience of drowning.

But the next two stanzas stand back and wonder, in a laconic way, whether this is in fact what we would hope for. Just supposing we went through the drama of falling off a ship or being swept away in a flood, wouldn't we want more made of our lives than this sudden flash? The question is obviously absurd (it is not imaginable that this would be our main preoccupation should we be unfortunate enough to face death by drowning). The narrator muses on, however, through several possibilities of a 'more leisurely review': the sense of browsing a family photo album; a short film or slide presentation; an essay or a 'model paragraph' of ourselves as hero of the plot of our life. It is almost as if he is meditating on the best way to plan a presentation of his own life, rather than trying to understand the processes of dying. Eventually the sequence of thoughts comes to a climax in an image redolent of a comic cartoon film, as the hapless hero has his eyebrows burned off as a sudden 'explosion of biography' goes off in his face. But then there is an afterthought that betrays the sense of pain there is in imagining that there will be very little said or written about one's life (as there could well be even about people who have made a significant contribution to the world through their lives or writings): 'nothing like the three large volumes you envisioned'.

There is a shift in the mood of the poem as we come to the last two stanzas. 'Survivors' are mentioned, presumably those who have been rescued from drowning or have otherwise returned from a near-death experience, and their witness to a sense of truth and light that seemed to surround it. But just as the reader thinks there may be some straightforward contemplation of what the experience may really be, it is as if the poet cannot resist sending up the 'bolt of truth' with its 'megalithic tonnage'. We are not given the space to take seriously the idea of 'ultimate Light', because it is immediately undercut by the next phrase 'before all the lights go out'. Tongue in cheek seems to be the default mode for facing the horror of dying, followed almost as an aside by what the narrator affirms is the banal and undramatic reality of our deaths: 'But if something does flash before your eyes/ as you go under, it will probably be a fish'. We are in the same territory as in the earlier poem by Roger McGough, where despite our fantasies of grandeur, our death does not really create a sensation when it comes to pass.

The thought continues on into the final stanza, like a body sinking through fathoms of water and assorted marine life that neither understands nor cares anything of the life that has fallen into the waves, 'having nothing to do with your life or your death'. The conclusion is bleak, if strangely soothing: there will be no sudden flash of understanding; there will be no drama; there will be no legacy of impressively ordered memorabilia (either compressed or in three volumes); and we ourselves will be past memory and caring in any case, as we become part of the natural 'disarray' at the bottom of the ocean. The poem's title turns out to be ironic: there is no 'art' associated with drowning, in any sense of the word: no artwork of memory will be created; no way of approaching one's fate will prove to be more skilful than another. A poem that is apparently speculating about what it is really like to drown turns out to be more about our disappointing – or non-existent – legacy in people's memories.

Aubade

I work all day, and get half-drunk at night.
Waking at four to soundless dark, I stare.
In time the curtain-edges will grow light.
Till then I see what's really always there:
Unresting death, a whole day nearer now,
Making all thought impossible but how
And where and when I shall myself die.
Arid interrogation: yet the dread
Of dying, and being dead,
Flashes afresh to hold and horrify.

The mind blanks at the glare. Not in remorse
– The good not done, the love not given, time
Torn off unused – nor wretchedly because
An only life can take so long to climb
Clear of its wrong beginnings, and may never;
But at the total emptiness for ever,
The sure extinction that we travel to
And shall be lost in always. Not to be here,
Not to be anywhere,
And soon; nothing more terrible, nothing more true.

This is a special way of being afraid
No trick dispels. Religion used to try,
That vast, moth-eaten musical brocade
Created to pretend we never die,
And specious stuff that says *No rational being
Can fear a thing it will not feel*, not seeing
That this is what we fear – no sight, no sound,
No touch or taste or smell, nothing to think with,
Nothing to love or link with,
The anaesthetic from which none come round.

And so it stays just on the edge of vision,
A small unfocused blur, a standing chill
That slows each impulse down to indecision.
Most things may never happen: this one will,
And realisation of it rages out

In furnace-fear when we are caught without
People or drink. Courage is no good:
It means not scaring others. Being brave
Lets no one off the grave.
Death is no different whined at than withstood.

Slowly light strengthens, and the room takes shape.
It stands plain as a wardrobe, what we know,
Have always known, know that we can't escape,
Yet can't accept. One side will have to go.
Meanwhile telephones crouch, getting ready to ring
In locked-up offices, and all the uncaring
Intricate rented world begins to rouse.
The sky is white as clay, with no sun.
Work has to be done.
Postmen like doctors go from house to house.

Philip Larkin

This is perhaps one of the bleakest contemporary poems ever written about the fear of death. In contrast with earlier eras, where fear of dying was likely to be associated with worrying about the fate of one's eternal soul, and the threat of hell, Larkin's poem explores, with a brutal directness, the narrator's horror at the thought of the absolute personal annihilation he is convinced he faces. Written not long after the death of Larkin's mother, the tone of the poem may well reflect the kind of insomniac depression that can attend the early months of bereavement. Its flat, despairing tone is interesting to compare with other famous reflections on the sheer fear of death, for instance Claudio's speech in Shakespeare's *Measure for Measure*: 'Ay, but to die, and go we know not where' (Act 3, scene 1). Though it proclaims that any kind of earthly life, however stricken by poverty or pain, is better than the prospect of death, this speech nevertheless has an energy and excitement about it that is completely lacking in the Larkin poem.

Typically for Larkin's poetry, 'Aubade' – an ironically 'poetic' title for the horrors the period just pre-dawn can inspire – combines a highly conversational tone with an extremely subtle use of rhyme and metre. There is a steady iambic five-beat line (the metre often used by Shakespeare as it is so suitable for spoken English), which is only varied, for emphasis, in the penultimate line of each stanza. The regular end-rhyme scheme (ABABCCDEED) is so well achieved that the reader can fail to notice it. Apparently casual, this poem is in fact a carefully organized vehicle for contemplating the existential abyss.

Larkin catches brilliantly the grey repetitiveness of deeply troubling thoughts that overpower the sleepless at four in the morning: the unclosed, staring eyes waiting for the advent of light around the edges of the curtains; the conviction that what is apprehended in the small hours is 'what's really always there'. This is 'Unresting death, a whole day nearer now'. This displacing of the adjective (for in reality it is the speaker himself who is 'unresting') makes the power of death seem inexorable. It is as if the fact of death, having been stared at by the speaker, stares back like an interrogator flashing a fierce light to terrify a suspect. 'The mind blanks at the glare.'

The second stanza (like the circling gloomy thoughts themselves) goes around and around the prospect of nothingness, and what that means. It carefully distinguishes the precise nature of that dread, explaining that it is not the same as remorse for what has been done or, more importantly, not done with the time allotted for a life. And yet the detailed mention of these regrets has some poignancy: the difficulty of getting clear of 'wrong beginnings'; love not offered; and, in a bleak and powerful image of sheer waste, 'time/ Torn off unused'. The stanza is stuffed with negatives, endlessly repeated: 'not', 'never', 'nothing'.

The third stanza gives short shrift to whatever ideologies there are that might offer any comfort in the face of *timor mortis*: religion – which is denied even the validity of something with contemporary salience (it only 'used to try') – or rationalist philosophy, rejected as 'specious stuff'. Again the procession of negatives calls up the agonizing prospect of nothingness, an absence of human bodily senses or intellect. (This part of the poem recalls the Shakespearean depiction of very old age in *As You Like It*: 'sans eyes, sans teeth, sans taste, sans everything'.) Larkin captures the very texture of despair: repetitive, gloomy, but with an answer for every objection, deadly but utterly reasonable.

The fourth stanza seems to be summing up the problem, creating a little more sense of distance from the horror. The fear is now 'A small unfocused blur, a standing chill' that dominates only 'when we are caught without/ People or drink'. And yet despair continues, as the narrator points out that there is no demeanour we can adopt (not even courage) that can affect our situation. 'Being brave/ Lets no one off the grave'. This is a familiar thought for anyone who faces terminal illness or watches another do so, since we keep having to remind ourselves that we cannot negotiate with death via good behaviour. But there is a certain courage in exposing this so honestly.

Finally, though the poem offers absolutely no resolution of the problem (being convinced that there is none), the daylight arrives, as it always does after even the worst night. There is a kind of comfort to be derived from the structures and definition of the day's routines and furniture. Instead of being imagined as an interrogation lamp or a furnace, the unacceptable fact of our mortality is just 'plain as a wardrobe', and 'Work has to be done'. The accoutrements of the day are threatening (telephones like crouching predators; postmen like harbingers of serious illness) or closed and blank (sky 'white as clay', 'locked-up offices'). It is, in the psyche of this narrator, an 'uncaring/ Intricate rented world' – a world temporarily occupied and never owned, by lives made pointless by having to leave it.

Lines: 'I Am'

I am – yet what I am, none cares or knows;
My friends forsake me like a memory lost:
I am the self-consumer of my woes –
They rise and vanish in oblivion's host
Like shadows in love-frenzied stifled throes –
And yet I am and live – like vapours tossed

Into the nothingness of scorn and noise,
Into the living sea of waking dreams
Where there is neither sense of life or joys
But the vast shipwreck of my life's esteems;
Even the dearest that I love the best
Are strange – nay, rather, stranger than the rest.

I long for scenes where man hath never trod,
A place where woman never smiled or wept,
There to abide with my Creator, God,
And sleep as I in childhood sweetly slept,
Untroubling and untroubled where I lie,
The grass below – above, the vaulted sky.

John Clare

This is perhaps the most famous of John Clare's poems, and it is interesting to compare it with the previous one, Larkin's 'Aubade'. Both texts seem to emerge from a sense of despair, and yet their contemplation of death itself could hardly be more different.

Clare was a contemporary of John Keats, and at one time his poetry actually outsold that of Keats. Born the son of an agricultural labourer, Clare grew up in serious poverty in the village of Helpston near Peterborough, then part of Northamptonshire. His education was limited but he was a bookish child whose parents were rather alarmed by his interest in writing his own poetry. Clare was deeply observant of the natural world of his surroundings, and unlike some Romantic poets was actually knowledgeable about plant and bird life. He resented the destructive changes that came about in the countryside as a result of the agricultural revolution and the enclosure of common land, and his poetry frequently returns to his childhood memories of familiarity and freedom among the countryside he loved.

He had ambitions to be widely published, and initially he was all the rage, being presented to the public as a 'peasant poet', a genuine Romantic natural voice. But he never found a comfortable place within the literary world and he continued to need to earn a living through a variety of labouring work. Eventually the fashion for his writing collapsed and his fame waned, though he always continued to write. At the same time, he was not at home among ordinary labourers, who apparently were uneasy in his company in case they ended up in his poems. His love life was complex. Though he married and had children, he never forgot his first love, Mary Joyce, whose father had forbidden him to woo her.

Clare experienced ill health throughout his life, including malnutrition in childhood and possibly 'fen ague', a variety of endemic malarial illness. In the latter decades of his life, Clare suffered from long periods of mental illness, and spent some time in the Northampton County Asylum. Although when admitted his insanity was described as arising 'after years addicted to poetical prosings', he was in fact encouraged to write under a humane regime, and 'I Am' dates from this period of his life.

So in a sense this is a poem of 'madness', and the burden of the first two stanzas witnesses to the deep isolation so often experienced by those who are mentally ill. Yet it is by no means a raving text, but a carefully controlled exploration of this condition, with a regular rhythmic metre and rhyme scheme, each verse coming to rest in a couplet. The narrator of the poem is self-aware. There are religious echoes: the title 'I am', repeated four times in the first verse, is the traditional mysterious name that the God of the Exodus, revealed to Moses, gives himself (Exodus 3.14). Later, in John's Gospel, Jesus is shown using this phrase about himself (John 8.58). The second line also has biblical resonances, as the psalms often speak of friends forsaking the one who is lamenting. This initial assertion of identity is both minimalist (a man who is nothing but an isolated creature who merely exists) and massive (a creature made in the image of God).

But then the 'woes' threaten to overwhelm. It is no coincidence that the third 'I am' – 'I am the self-consumer of my woes' – has become a proverbial saying, so accurate is it as a description of despair and its cyclical self-feeding destructiveness. The vague and evanescent attacking thoughts 'rise and vanish', expressing how powerful and yet how hard to pin down they are. But the fourth 'I am' asserts itself even when the speaker is haunted by distressing memories, and by painful internal struggles he cannot quite define: 'And yet I am'.

The second stanza, with similar precision, charts the confusion about reality that the narrator is suffering: 'the nothingness of scorn and noise'; 'the living sea of waking dreams'. Then, as now, the mentally ill suffered huge stigma for their condition as well as the distress of the mind itself. Unable to access either joy or a sense of pleasure in life, the narrator is aware only of the failure of all that he has attempted: 'the vast shipwreck of my life's esteems'. The image brilliantly continues that of the 'living sea' of the confusion that he suffers. The last two lines explore his distance from loved ones (who called the doctors in). Here the rhythm of the text is broken as he states and restates the situation, reflecting the heartache involved.

But then the mood changes, and the narrator's thoughts are turned towards a desire for solitude deliberately chosen. The place of freedom is envisaged 'where man hath never trod', apparently a rural wilderness such as he explored in childhood. Playing on the double meanings of 'man' he then introduces 'woman', but the focus is on the smiles and tears of women – the matters of the heart that were for Clare so tortuous. And then he greets a life with 'my Creator, God', imagined with childlike simplicity and assurance, and we become aware that he is choosing not the world outside the walls of the asylum but the sweet sleep of the grave. Death is foreseen as the closure of his troubles, whether happening to him or caused by him. As an image of a gentle and longed-for death, this has seldom been bettered, and appropriately recalls the freedom of childhood, all constraints and enclosures gone: 'The grass below – above, the vaulted sky.'

Smile, Death

Smile, Death, see I smile as I come to you
Straight from the road and the moor that I leave behind,
Nothing on earth to me was like this wind-blown space,
Nothing was like the road, but at the end there was a vision or a face
    And the eyes were not always kind.

  Smile, Death, as you fasten the blades to my feet for me,
On, on let us skate past the sleeping willows dusted with snow;
Fast, fast down the frozen stream, with the moor and the road and
    the vision behind,
(Show me your face, why the eyes are kind!)
And we will not speak of life or believe in it or remember it as we go.

Charlotte Mew

Charlotte Mew was another poet who suffered from the effects of mental illness in her family, and latterly in her own life. One of seven children, her father died having made very little provision for those left behind. Three siblings died in childhood, and two were committed to mental institutions. Charlotte and her remaining sister, Anne, both vowed not to marry (so as not to pass on any insanity), but it seems likely that in any case Charlotte's passionate life was orientated towards women. She wore men's clothes and kept her hair short. When her sister Anne was diagnosed with liver cancer, Charlotte fell into a deep depression and eventually took her own life by drinking Lysol.

This poem forms an interesting comparison with the earlier poem by her quoted in this book ('In the Fields', p. 7), in which she expresses an intense commitment to the transient beauties of this world. But it is also in marked contrast with the previous poems by Larkin and Clare, which envisage death as horrific annihilation or a comforting childhood embrace. Here, there is apparently a fierce enjoyment in envisaging an encounter with Death, imagined as a companion ice skater, racing her in her journey towards an unknown infinity.

It is a brief but arresting dramatic monologue, with the last four lines of each stanza having a rhyming pattern BCCB. The lines are typically long and ranging, mirroring the sense of onward, flowing movement such as fast ice skaters might achieve. There is also a theme of facial expression which recurs in different ways.

The first stanza addresses Death, boldly proclaiming the narrator's own courage and resolutely cheerful demeanour as she approaches: 'see I smile as I come to you'. (One imagines Death as a person who will find this unexpected, being more accustomed to deep reluctance to leave this life in those who are summoned out of it.) In contrast to the rather domestic landscape of 'In the Fields', this narrator is apparently passionately attached to the wild and wide open spaces of wind-blown moorland and the road that gave access to its freedom and emptiness. Yet the speaker seems ready to relinquish this earthly territory, where the horizon seemed to include 'a vision or a face' whose eyes were 'not always kind'. Perhaps the reference is to some kind of anxiety about a judging deity at the end of life. Charlotte Mew wrestled with religious faith, being attracted to traditional Catholicism but also exploring some of the more experimental religious ideas of her day, such as the emphasis on the humanity of Christ and his radical acceptance of women.

In the second stanza, the narrator is abandoning the road and taking to skating on the 'frozen stream' (much more risky but potentially faster and more exciting), and imagines Death actually fastening the blades on her feet for her. (Ice skates of this period could be temporarily attached to the ordinary winter boots people wore.) Now her view of the landscape has changed perspective and it is the willow trees either side of the river that she notices – 'the sleeping willows dusted with snow'. In a very few words the poet establishes the clear visual images of the trees: asleep because in their winter dormancy, perhaps drooping as some willows do, like dozing creatures. But there is also the sense that nothing the narrator witnesses is aware of the intense excitement she is experiencing by dancing with Death in this way. One is reminded of the Emily Dickinson poem 'Because I could not stop for Death', where a similarly courtly (if ominous) journey is being shared, which takes the speaker past and beyond all that she has known.

It is as if the speed increases, as the landscape flashes past and is now behind her. Not only the road but also the 'vision' she previously entertained are now in the past, and in the bracketed line that follows it is as if the speaker turns to her companion to check what his facial expression is now. To her delight and surprise, 'why the eyes are kind!' The process of going with Death willingly seems to be comfortable, or at least enjoyable, as in a developing flirtation or risky friendship. The speaker seems to fling all caution to the winds and simply revel in it.

The last line is extraordinary: 'And we will not speak of life or believe in it or remember it as we go.' Everything has been reversed. It is common to resist speaking about death, and to act as if we don't believe in it. Finding joy in life is often contrasted with remembering our mortality. But here it is life that is the thing not believed in, and death carries the sense of speed, delight and enjoyable risk.

So the poem seems to be a forthright welcoming of death, and yet it does not actually sound depressed or suicidal in any way. Its strong bodily image of pleasure in speed gives it a feeling of robust acceptance: that if we have to go, this is the spirit in which to encounter our death.

Sonnet 73

That time of year thou mayst in me behold
When yellow leaves, or none, or few, do hang
Upon those boughs which shake against the cold,
Bare ruined choirs where late the sweet birds sang;
In me thou see'st the twilight of such day
As after sunset fadeth in the west,
Which by and by black night doth take away,
Death's second self, that seals up all in rest;
In me thou see'st the glowing of such fire
That on the ashes of his youth doth lie,
As the death-bed, whereon it must expire,
Consumed with that which it was nourished by.
  This thou perceiv'st, which makes thy love more strong,
  To love that well, which thou must leave ere long.

William Shakespeare

The last two poems in this section take as central the theme of *memento mori*, not as a religious practice or in order to explore existential despair, but in the pursuit of romantic love. Shakespeare's sonnets constantly rework a theme that was deeply familiar around the court he flourished in. The speaker seeks to persuade the recipient of the sonnet that, since age and death will inevitably come to all, even to those who are currently young and desirable, it is important to love each other as well as we can right now. There is usually an undercurrent that the speaker has some persuading to do, as perhaps he does not currently feel that his love is fully reciprocated. Often this approach is a rather manipulative argument that a male speaker uses towards a woman (pointing out that her beauty, which she denies him the right to enjoy, is not actually going to last all that long). However, this poem stands in a sequence that seems to be addressed to a young man, and in any case Shakespeare rings the changes of this traditional approach in many and subtle ways. This particular sonnet is agreed by many to be an outstanding example of the form.

Shakespeare worked with the sonnet in a distinctive way that has come to be referred to as 'Shakespearean' because of his practice. Instead of consisting of an eight-line octet, introducing a theme or a dilemma, and then moving on to the sestet, which resolves the theme or provides an interesting twist on it, he uses three four-line quatrains (which rhyme alternate lines), which build up the poem's argument; then the theme is resolved in a final couplet with an adjacent end-rhyme that adds emphasis to the final two lines.

The poem does not immediately address or describe the beloved to whom it is written, but instead throws the attention back on the state of mind and heart of the lover who is speaking – a condition that may be clearly seen by the beloved, if he pays attention. Three times, the narrator repeats some variation of the phrase 'In me thou see'st'. And we are immediately flung into autumn, and the dying of the year (a season that resonates with the reality of human mortality). With extraordinarily artful simplicity he describes the state of the autumn trees, with their 'yellow leaves, or none, or few' hanging there. The word order is counter-intuitive, suggesting a gaze that wanders over the different trees in their threadbare or almost empty state. It is late autumn, not the glorious stage; and the denuded branches 'shake against the cold'. This image suggests a rough wind but also introduces the sense of human suffering as winter approaches.

But the autumnal season is firmly located within the narrator, just as if it is as visible to the eye as the weather around. What 'thou mayst in me behold' is precisely 'Bare ruined choirs where late the sweet birds sang'. This line is packed with resonance. Having been prepared by the image of the naked, shivering boughs, we are invited to see the tree branches (no longer any protection to the summer birds that used to roost and sing in them) as being like the long, parallel choir stalls of ruined churches, now exposed to wind and weather, where the monks or possibly choirboys used to sing sweet church music. Given how relatively recently the Tudor dynasty had put into effect the destruction of hundreds of monasteries and their chapels, deliberately creating ruins of the old religion, this is a politically daring image, drawing as it does on the poignant sense of loss it was probably not expedient to bear witness to in Shakespeare's age. This sense of being laid bare and ruined in his heart and body is what the speaker of the sonnet alleges he is suffering – and it should be evident to an attentive lover.

The second quatrain introduces a new image of himself, as someone for whom darkness is closing in at day's end, which, of course, happens increasingly early as autumn draws on. The narrator speaks of the 'twilight', the fading of the sunset in the west, the gradual capture of the light by the arrival of the night. These are images of age: perhaps the speaker was acutely conscious that he is older than his beloved and therefore his life is well past the zenith. Again, the quatrain ends in a stunning line: 'Death's second self, that seals up all in rest'. It is a traditional idea that sleeping is a sort of gentle practice run for dying (see Herbert's 'Death' on p. 148), but here the poet has left it uncertain whether it is sleep or night itself that mirrors death. The line is full of ominous sibilants, and the first three words, 'Death's second self', if read out loud, are quite thick and difficult to say together; you have to slow down to get your mouth around the clustered consonants. This gives emphasis to the image, as does the assonance of similar vowel sounds.

The third quatrain has yet another image, that of a fire (again, this is appropriate at the end of a cold autumn day that has slipped into night). The first two images of the speaker's self are about pain and age; this one implies passion. And yet it is the glowing of a fire that has reached an advanced stage. When wood is burnt, the fire becomes progressively a bed of ashes beneath newly placed logs. The ash bed retains its heat, and the new logs will therefore take fire even more readily than those that were initially set alight. At the same time, the later logs, because they burn more fiercely, will be consumed more quickly, because of the hot ashes that represent the fire's 'youth'. The narrator pinpoints how his love, which he suggests is burning more strongly because it is embedded in the passionate feelings of his youth, must eventually (through death) be 'Consumed with that which it was nourished by'.

Finally the couplet attempts to clinch the matter. Having argued that these truths about himself are transparent to a lover, he asserts 'This thou perceiv'st, which makes thy love more strong'. The reader may feel that this is a lover's powerful wish that it should be the case, rather than self-evident truth. Similarly with the final line, which encapsulates the rather manipulative punchline of the argument: I am going to die and you will lose me, so love me well while you still can. It is interesting that the poet uses the word 'leave' rather than lose; perhaps he is sowing a doubt, in spite of his protestations, about exactly how reliable his beloved may be in his affections.

When You are Old

When you are old and grey and full of sleep,
And nodding by the fire, take down this book,
And slowly read, and dream of the soft look
Your eyes had once, and of their shadows deep;

How many loved your moments of glad grace,
And loved your beauty with love false or true,
But one man loved the pilgrim soul in you,
And loved the sorrows of your changing face;

And bending down beside the glowing bars,
Murmur, a little sadly, how Love fled
And paced upon the mountains overhead
And hid his face amid a crowd of stars.

W. B. Yeats

Yeats' famous love poem to Maud Gonne is in a similar tradition to the sonnet of Shakespeare's, in that the speaker uses the idea of his death to provide a context for his love now. Indeed, in this poem the speaker is imagining that he is already departed, and the love relationship is remembered and reassessed in the poignancy of hindsight. But it is a truncated sonnet, omitting the final couplet that usually seeks to resolve the matter explored. It is all the more powerful for that, especially when the poem is compared with the sixteenth-century sonnet by Ronsard it is apparently based on: 'Quand vous serez bien vieille, au soir, à la chandelle' (When you are very old, in the evenings, by candlelight), written to Hélène in 1587. Some have described Yeats' version of it as a free paraphrase, but really it is a quite new poem, drawing on the power of the earlier underlying tradition.

Ronsard's sonnet was (like many of Shakespeare's sonnets in his more arrogant moods) actually more a celebration of his own lasting greatness as a writer than a depiction of the love of his life. His poem stresses the great age of his once beloved, and the picture isn't gentle; she is 'une vieille accroupie' (a hunched/crippled old woman). The evening of her life is spent reciting her lover's verses while marvelling that Ronsard himself used to celebrate her beauty during the short time she enjoyed it. Her tired old servants will rise up and bless her solely because they realize she is murmuring the name of Ronsard (who, sadly, is now a phantom taking his repose among the myrtle trees). And then he gets to his manipulative point, namely, how deeply she will regret his love and her proud disdain for his advances; it is time to snatch life's joys ('les roses de la vie') before the moment passes for ever. It is really all about the poet.

Yeats' poem starts similarly ('When you are old and grey and full of sleep') but continues in a rather different vein. Yes, his beloved is imagined nodding by the hearth in her old age, and is invited to 'take down this book' with his verses in (at least she isn't expected, as in Ronsard, to be so obsessed with him that she can recite them by heart). But what she goes on to think about is not her lover's fame or even her own departed beauty that inspired his writing. It is her own expression of love in her eyes when she looked at him. Of course, this is his memory of her, but to speak of it will surely make that expression appear once more; it does not matter that her face will be old.

The second quatrain recalls not that the poet's love for her was her one claim to fame, rather, it celebrates her capacity to inspire the love of many men, not just by her beauty but by her 'glad grace'. The beauty may have been in the past but the poem does not despise the woman for having lost it; indeed, beauty itself is a mixed blessing as it attracts 'love false or true'. Only now does he state his own claims on her heart: 'one man loved the pilgrim soul in you'; who would not rather be loved for this rather than outward appearance? And again it is her expression that is loved, whether glad or sorrowful; not a static beauty, but a 'changing face'.

Finally, the poem envisages the woman not racked by regrets but just murmuring 'a little sadly', of how 'Love fled'. In this poem, we are not told whether it was the speaker who did not have the courage to press his suit, or whether she reciprocated his love but death took him early. We know that Yeats' pursuit of Maud Gonne, the woman he saw as his Muse, was unsuccessful; she turned him down several times, after which he approached her daughter – who also, sensibly, rejected him. But this rather murky biographical drama doesn't intrude in the poem. I wonder if the capitalized Love refers to the god of love, Eros, who through an extraordinary passion introduced the beloved in the poem to a dimension of life that partook of divinity. The reference here could be to the myth of Psyche and Eros, since the attraction there was the beloved's 'pilgrim soul'. Psyche was loved by the Greek god of love, but it was a love celebrated wholly in the dark; she was forbidden to see his face. Yet she could not resist lighting the lamp one day, and she was punished by losing her lover, whom she then endlessly searched for without success. Certainly the last two lines of the poem, profoundly romantic beyond anything in Ronsard's original, suggest a divinity who hides his face. It has gone beyond the ordinary human lover who is the speaker of the poem, into the realm of transcendence – what Yeats elsewhere refers to as 'the cloths of heaven'.

So Yeats' poem does not hammer home any lessons about seizing life's joys (and going to bed with me) before death intervenes. It lingers as the memory of a deeply significant attachment of love that transcends death.

ACTUAL CRISIS

What the Doctor Said

He said it doesn't look good
he said it looks bad in fact real bad
he said I counted thirty-two of them on one lung before
I quit counting them
I said I'm glad I wouldn't want to know
about any more being there than that
he said are you a religious man do you kneel down
in forest groves and let yourself ask for help
when you come to a waterfall
mist blowing against your face and arms
do you stop and ask for understanding at those moments
I said not yet but I intend to start today
he said I'm real sorry he said
I wish I had some other kind of news to give you
I said Amen and he said something else
I didn't catch and not knowing what else to do
and not wanting him to have to repeat it
and me to have to fully digest it
I just looked at him
for a minute and he looked back it was then
I jumped up and shook hands with this man who'd just given me
something no one else on earth had ever given me
I may even have thanked him habit being so strong

Raymond Carver

If the poems in the previous section explore the process of fantasiz-
ing about one's own death, perhaps fearfully, perhaps in order to
imagine or manipulate the reactions of others, this section of the
book is about responding to an immediate crisis. There is a great
deal of difference between thinking about personal mortality in
principle, when you are feeling perfectly well, and contemplating it
when the doctor has delivered a terminal diagnosis, or when someone
you love is manifestly dying now.

This poem by Raymond Carver is about receiving a terminal diag-
nosis, and it was written shortly before his death from lung cancer.
It addresses the numbness and shock of receiving such news, and
pinpoints (in an almost comic way) how someone getting a diagnosis

like this has absolutely no idea how to behave in such circumstances, so ends up being scrupulously polite – or at least, that is their hazy memory of the encounter: 'I may even have thanked him habit being so strong'.

Everything about how the poem is written echoes this sense of confusion. There is not a single example of punctuation, so one reads it breathlessly, not knowing quite when to pause – just as someone in that situation might pour out his story at home the evening after seeing the doctor. The whole narrative is conveyed by a series of 'he said', 'I said' clauses, the traditional way to retell shocking news. But it is well known that it is incredibly difficult to remember exactly the details of a medical consultation when the news is difficult, and close examination suggests that the speaker's memory has already distorted 'what the doctor said' via the filter of his own panicky feelings.

For although it is possible that the doctor remarked 'it doesn't look good', it seems slightly improbable that he would go on to emphasize the situation as 'bad in fact real bad' (even if things were, as they seem to be, dire). Neither is the exchange about exactly how many tumours feature on the lungs really plausible, so that the doctor allegedly 'quit counting them'. However, this sets up the first absurd response from the patient, as he desperately tries to produce an adequately polite, harmonizing reply to what is effectively a clear sentence of death: 'I'm glad I wouldn't want to know/ about any more being there than that'.

The remembered dialogue then shoots off into a wilder exchange – most unlikely to have occurred between doctor and patient, but very likely to have happened internally, as the terrible news suddenly catapults the speaker into contemplating ultimate matters of life, death, prayer and whether there is a God who can help in this crisis. It is as if he has been asked to account for himself: 'are you a religious man'. The notion of kneeling down in the woods and begging for help has a certain over-the-top religious romanticism about it, which is highlighted as he reveals that he has never done any such thing 'but I intend to start today' (since, finally, prayer seems to be an urgent necessity). But it does seem that the detail of the 'waterfall/ mist blowing against your face and arms', which connects humanity in a fierce and bracing way with the natural world, is an image that the poet has frequently used before.

The doctor's apology that there is no better news to give is conveyed as if it were part of a ritual bidding and response, to which the patient replies 'Amen'. Then something is said that the patient didn't catch, and (as too easily happens in the intensely brief time one has with a consultant) hasn't the courage to ask him to repeat. The failed exchange at this point reflects the patient's sense that it is absolutely beyond him to digest any further information (to the extent that he has in fact digested any of this 'fully'). It has taken several lines for the speaker to explain that he doesn't know what was said then or what he should do in response; and these lines of non-information leave the reader in a similarly nonplussed situation.

There is a convincing moment of silence when the patient and his helpless but sympathetic doctor just look at each other, as the information about a terminal diagnosis sinks in wordlessly. Finally the speaker takes dramatic charge of the encounter in the only way that occurs to him, by leaping to his feet and shaking the doctor's hand, as if in gratitude for what he has done. Interestingly, this is not named as delivering a death sentence, but as 'something no one else on earth had ever given me'. This is completely true: the exchange must be unique, and although there is, of course, an element of irony about the value of such a gift, I believe there is a level at which the narrator is partly serious. Whether or not he rushes away to get on his knees to a God he has never previously prayed to, he has received information that reveals to him in the most piercingly poignant way how deeply he feels connected to this life, and how unprepared he is to deal with the news that his time is so short. Although the tone is humorous, the whole poem conveys an authentic encounter with reality that readers (however much we think we 'know' that we too will die one day) can't help being jolted by.

She Replies to Carmel's Letter

It was a mild Christmas, the small fine rain kept washing over,
so I coated myself in plastics,
walked further than I could manage.
Leave me now, I'd say, and when they had tramped ahead
I'd sit myself down on a stone or the side of a high grass ditch,
or anywhere – like a duck in a puddle –
I'd rest a bit, then I would muddle around
the winding boreens that crawled the headland.

Sometimes, waterproofed and not caring,
I'd sit in a road that was really a stream-bed,
being and seeing from down where the hare sees,
sitting in mud and in wetness,
the world rising hummocky round me,
the sudden grass on the skyline,
the fence post, with the earth run from under it,
swinging like a hanged man.

Then I would want to praise
the ease of low wet things, the song of them, like a child's low drone,
and praising I'd watch how the water flowing the track
is clear, so I might not see it
but for the scrumpled place where it runs on a scatter of grit,
the flat, swelled place where it slides itself over a stone.
So now, when you write that you labour to strip off the layers,
and there might not, under them, be anything at all,

I remember that time, and I wish you had sat there, with me,
your skin fever-hot, the lovely wet coldness of winter mud
on your red, uncovered hands,
knowing it's all in the layers,
the flesh on the bones, the patterns that the bones push
upwards onto the flesh. So, you will see how it is with me,
and that sometimes even sickness is generous
and takes you by the hand and sits you
beside things you would otherwise have passed over.

Kerry Hardie

This poem is explicitly written as a reply to a letter whose contents we do not know, but it reads as if the narrator of the poem is writing to a friend, who is suffering a serious health problem (perhaps cancer?). She has written because the narrator has gone through something similar. Death, or the fear of death, is not specifically mentioned, but the suffering involved is sufficiently major to invite the kind of self-examination about ultimate things that the speaker in the previous poem by Raymond Carver has suddenly seen the point of: 'you write that you labour to strip off the layers'.

The poem begins with the narrator's memory of her own period of struggle with the body, which may have been recovering from chemotherapy or other treatment. In the very first line, the motif of wetness – a sort of healing wetness – is introduced: 'the small fine rain kept washing over'. Recognizably typical weather in Hardie's Irish context, the rain is described in ways that are positive. The weather, though late December, is mild; the rain is 'fine', and its activity feels cleansing. I wonder if there is an echo of that famous ancient anonymous poem, 'Western wind, when wilt thou blow/ The small rain down can rain.' The narrator seems at ease with, or at least resigned to, her relative weakness compared with her companions who want a Christmas walk. She does not just find herself faltering, but plans how to manage her weakness, protecting herself with comprehensive waterproofs, knowing that she is walking further than she can really manage, and comfortably dismissing more energetic folk when she needs to rest herself. There is a strong contrast between the healthy, as they 'tramped ahead', and herself, as she 'would muddle around'. But she is not frustrated or self-accusing; she is 'like a duck in a puddle' (notice the rhyme with 'muddle'); and, like a duck, appears to embrace the wetness in an unusual way.

The second stanza shifts the perspective arrestingly, and we understand what all the waterproofs are for. She simply has to sit down now, as she knew she would have to. 'Not caring' reflects both the point of the extra protective layer and also a freedom from ordinary social rules, which determine that it is just very odd behaviour for humans to sit down in the middle of a wet road. But once she is down there, sitting 'in a road which was really a stream-bed', certain insights and perspectives become available to her. Suddenly she sees the landscape 'from down where the hare sees'. It is an interesting choice of animal to identify with; hares are traditionally sacred in pagan Celtic tradition, and have been thought of as 'shape-shifters'. But the point is that everything looks different from low down, where people don't usually sit. (Hares crouch right down in the grass to hide themselves.) Instead of distant hills she sees hummocks looming above her, and the skyline becomes the grass right next to her. She sees the dodgy fence post from beneath, noticing why it is 'swinging like a hanged man' (the image is threatening); the endless rain has washed away the earth it was set in.

But the mood swings away from ominous to celebratory; the speaker wants to 'praise/ the ease of low wet things', and she focuses on a particular observation of the distinctive flow of water across the uneven country road, which she would not have noticed from higher up. She sees the detail of the 'scrumpled place where it runs on a scatter of grit,/ the flat, swelled place where it slides itself over a stone'; and we realize that this is an exact description of the routes that copious rainwater does seek out (as if intentionally) across roads that have no urban drains. But we probably haven't attended to it before. Somehow this new 'seeing from below' becomes a point of connection with the friend's letter, whose illness has asked of her a stripping off of layers of herself.

The final stanza brings together her friend's current suffering with the speaker's memory of sudden insight during her own period of weakness, and the place it brought her to. It is full of awareness of the body, some of it uncomfortable ('your skin fever-hot', 'your red, uncovered hands', some of it oddly comforting ('the lovely wet coldness of winter mud'), and it ends with the austere but, in the context of the poem, convincing testimony to the power of serious suffering to introduce unexpected wisdom. The image is quite tender, even maternal: 'sometimes even sickness is generous/ and takes you by the hand and sits you/ beside things you would otherwise have passed over.'

Hymn to God, my God, in my Sickness

Since I am coming to that holy room,
  Where, with thy choir of saints for evermore,
I shall be made thy music; as I come
    I tune the instrument here at the door,
    And what I must do then, think here before.

Whilst my physicians by their love are grown
  Cosmographers, and I their map, who lie
Flat on this bed, that by them may be shown
    That this is my south-west discovery
    Per fretum febris, by these straits to die,

I joy, that in these straits, I see my west;
  For, though their currents yield return to none,
What shall my west hurt me? As west and east
    In all flat maps (and I am one) are one,
    So death doth touch the resurrection.

Is the pacific sea my home? Or are
  The eastern riches? Is Jerusalem?
Anyan, and Magellan, and Gibraltar,
    All straits, and none but straits, are ways to them,
    Whether where Japhet dwelt, or Cham, or Sem.

We think that Paradise and Calvary,
  Christ's Cross, and Adam's tree, stood in one place;
Look Lord, and find both Adams met in me;
    As the first Adam's sweat surrounds my face,
    May the last Adam's blood my soul embrace.

So, in his purple wrapped receive me, Lord,
  By these his thorns give me his other crown;
And as to others' souls I preached thy word,
    Be this my text, my sermon to mine own,
    Therefore that he may raise the Lord throws down.

John Donne

Donne's earliest biographer, Izaak Walton, suggests that this poem
was written only eight days before Donne's death in 1631. However,
others think that it may have been composed earlier, in 1623, when

he experienced a period of severe illness. Assuming that it is strongly autobiographical – and it reads as a genuine reflection on an experience of believing himself to have been very close to death – it is perhaps most likely to have been written after a degree of recovery from 'sickness unto death'. It has all the assurance and complexity of thought and construction that is typical of Donne's metaphysical poetry. It is written in iambic pentameter, with a very regular ABABB rhyme, and even when foreseeing death it plays with extravagant imaginative conceits (extended metaphors using unexpected ideas).

But the narrator's voice is that of one who is facing his imminent mortality, addressing his God in prayer. The first stanza begins with a poignant image of the dying man envisaging himself as a musician who is approaching an important performance. Heaven is like a 'holy room' where a chamber concert will be held, and where a choir will sing. In Donne's time, most music (apart from in cathedrals) would have been made in the quite intimate settings of people's homes. Many educated people would themselves play an instrument and get together socially with friends to make music. So there is a lovely domesticity about this prospect, although also a certain fearfulness. The narrator speaks of tuning his instrument 'here at the door', as if he needs to be completely ready to enter the room before he is asked to play. The image relates to the need for reflection and preparation before death, but there is an additional twist: the narrator's body is seen as the 'instrument', and his whole self will not just make music but 'be made thy music'. So we can see the ravages and discomfort of bodily illness as a kind of tuning-up process that is stretching but essential.

The second stanza shifts back to the sick patient flat on his bed with fever, and begins a long and sustained image based on cartography, or map-making (part of the contemporary excitement about exploration and scientific discovery). The doctors, whose attention to the flattened patient is ironically described as 'love', are studying details of the patient's body as if it were a map on a table, yielding insights about areas of the world beyond most people's normal experience. They focus on 'straits' (later listed), which were crucial as gateways to whole new seas, and there is a deliberate pun on the word, in the sense of 'desperate straits', the gateway to death. The Latin tag '*Per fretum febris*' (via the straits of fever) gives this concept a humorous academic touch.

But the third stanza takes this ironic image and makes almost a credal statement out of it. The speaker takes up the common idea that to die is to travel to 'my west', but affirms his joy in seeing it before him on the map of his body. For given that flat maps are created from a world that is actually a globe, the distance between ultimate west and ultimate east (the place where the resurrection was revealed) is illusory; they become one and the same place. This is an idea that Donne uses in a sermon: 'paste that map upon a round body and then West and East are all one'. Just so, if we conform our lives to that of Christ (one of whose Advent titles is 'Oriens', the East), 'thy West is East'.

The next stanza is a further riff based on global exploration, as the speaker muses on where his true home can be found. 'Jerusalem' means both the actual place on the map and the heavenly Jerusalem, which is seen as the place of final gathering into the blessed saints of God (Revelation 21.2). Anyan is the Bering Straits, the North West passage. Magellan is the gateway to the Pacific, and Gibraltar the route to the Mediterranean and the Holy Land. Japhet, Cham and Sem refer to the sons of the biblical patriarch Noah, and according to legend they settled in Europe, Africa and Asia respectively. Encompassing the whole of the known world, the poem again states the inevitability of passing through 'straits' if a homeland is to be reached; and so it is with dying.

The fifth stanza returns to more familiar Christian teaching, exploring the tradition that the garden of Paradise (the place of the Fall) and Calvary (the place of Christ's crucifixion and therefore of redemption) stood in the same place. Both sites crucially involved a tree – or a cross made from a tree. Medieval Christianity made much of this idea, for example in the famous long poem 'The Dream of the Rood'. Whether this was believed in Donne's time as an actual or a metaphorical truth, he turns the idea into fervent prayer: 'Look Lord, and find both Adams met in me'. The 'both Adams' refer to the idea that Christ was like a second Adam, reversing the sin of the first Adam for our redemption (see Paul's discussion of this in 1 Corinthians 15). The couplet in this stanza presents a paradox that is both economic in expression and visceral in its imagery: 'As the first Adam's sweat surrounds my face,/ May the last Adam's blood my soul embrace.'

The 'sweat' conveys the patient's actual feverish sweats, but also refers to Adam's punishment, which is exclusion from Paradise and the necessity of hard work ('In the sweat of your face you shall eat bread', Genesis 3.19). The 'blood' is the salvific blood of Christ for the redemption of his soul.

The matter of his soul's eternal fate, which would have been the abiding concern of anyone facing death in Donne's age, begins the last stanza as the passionate prayer continues. Here the speaker uses imagery taken from the Passion narrative, which is the story of salvation. 'In his purple wrapped' refers to the blotchy, discoloured skin of the feverish patient, but also references the purple robe in which the soldiers mockingly clothed Jesus after his trial (Mark 15.17); 'these his thorns' refers to the pains of illness, but also the crown of thorns that was placed on Jesus' head. And finally there is the necessary humility of the famous preacher who, like anyone who preaches, must address himself first and last. Echoing many of the psalms of lament, which after much complaining finally affirm belief in a God who will raise the psalmist to life (such as Psalms 22, 31), he asserts that this current prostration before a final illness is necessary: 'Therefore that he may raise the Lord throws down.'

A hymn

Living with cancer and sauntering along a beach

On our familiar strand
our feet we lightly place:
we build our castle towers and walls
but leave behind no trace.

Relentlessly the sea
uncovers graves and stones,
reclaiming what we thought was ours,
our cells, our flesh, our bones.

The pincers of the crab
attack us from the side:
they drag us helpless, down and down,
through surf and ebbing tide.

Our journey to the west
cannot postpone the sea:
eternity soon swallows time,
land's end for you and me.

Our bodies' fibres part,
the thread of gold is drawn,
ourselves slimmed down for needle's eye,
yet into glory born(e).

Jim Cotter

This hymn, written a couple of years before Jim Cotter's death in 2013 from leukaemia, also takes travelling westward as a fitting image for the human pilgrimage towards death. Originally containing lines that tie the verse explicitly to the far west end of the North Wales Llyn peninsula, the text was revised by Cotter to make it more generally accessible and singable for Christians. Cotter, like the poet R. S. Thomas before him, exercised a ministry in his latter years in the church in Aberdaron, which for many generations has attracted pilgrims. Aberdaron is the little town where pilgrims have found accommodation before undertaking a rather risky boat journey across the turbulent sound of water to the island of Bardsey/Enlli. This island has had a history of pilgrimage since the sixth century, when monks began to live and worship there. It became the place of '20,000 saints' as it became popular to go and spend one's last days on the island and be buried there. Cotter's text is significant because the explicit contemplation of death and what lies beyond – commonplace among earlier generations of Christian poets and hymn-writers – has become really quite unusual during the last century or so.

The title of the poem places it as a cancer meditation 'sauntering along a beach'. To walk slowly along a beach is a traditional leisure activity, with possibilities for noticing and perhaps collecting treasured stones, shells, fossils or driftwood; and perhaps slow progress is the only kind of walk possible when living with a limiting disease. But Cotter probably also had in mind the popular (though disputed) derivation of the word 'saunter', which may have been applied to 'sainte-terrers' – people who were set on undertaking the pilgrimage to the Holy Land.

The text is written in a simple metre with an extra beat in the third line, and the second and fourth lines rhyme. This makes for an easy sing, and the words also have a simplicity, as the narrator contemplates the paring down of all that he is, in preparation for death. The first stanza places us on the beach; the 'castle towers and walls' imply the building of sandcastles, which are quintessentially temporary structures. Half the fun of building one is to watch the sea gradually advance and overwhelm the castle, making it collapse and dissolve. The implication is that human life (including the poet's) involves planting our feet lightly on a beach, and all that we construct in a lifetime actually leaves behind 'no trace'. We are asked to relinquish the pride and ambition that have built up a life's achievements.

The second stanza develops the sense of the relentless and destructive power of the sea. In that part of the coastline, erosion caused by the sea has indeed bitten into traditional shoreside graveyards. So it is not only the structures of ambition and self-protections ('castle towers and walls') that come down, but even our very graves might be opened. Cotter takes the thought into the even more intimate domain of our own bodies, 'reclaiming what we thought was ours,/ our cells, our flesh, our bones'. Many cancer sufferers feel that they are living with a condition that seems to have colonized their bodies and taken over the very structures that keep them alive.

The third stanza names the cancer through its traditional name, 'the crab' (as in the star sign of the crab, which is called Cancer). It is as if a horrific sea creature has emerged and is dragging us down into the tide of the sea that will drown us. Crabs do move and attack their prey in a characteristic sideways manner. What is implied is the way in which cancer as a disease seems to advance and take over in an unnoticed way until it can be too late. For some patients, whatever treatment is attempted fails to stall the process of being dragged down towards a death against which we are helpless. The fourth stanza sums up what is inevitable about human existence, whether or not cancer is the cause, namely that we are mortal and that our life will end with our death. Like the inescapable approach of the incoming tide, death will come to us and cannot be avoided or postponed. But the imagery, though fearful, is actually hopeful. What is 'land's end for you and me' (the reader is explicitly included for the first time) is not exactly an ending but a move into a larger reality: 'eternity soon swallows time'.

The final verse seems to turn the images of collapse and colonization into something much more precious. Although it is still the case that 'Our bodies' fibres part' – as they do during terminal illness and after death – what is drawn from them is like a 'thread of gold'. This is reminiscent perhaps of the sunlight effects in the landscape around the beach, whether shafts of light in the sky or reflected on the water. It is also an image of something very slender and delicate but made of pure gold – an essential part of our dying selves that may be drawn over into what comes next. The metaphor of the thread links with the 'needle's eye' in the next line, as if some beautiful tapestry, of which we are part, will be created by an unseen hand. But it also, of course, recalls Jesus' parable about the rich person who is less likely to enter the kingdom of heaven than a camel is to pass through the eye of a needle (Mark 10.25). So the shedding of personal ambition or pride in achievement, implied at the start of the poem, is affirmed as necessary as death itself is faced. Cotter's stunning phrase 'ourselves slimmed down' conveys both the gauntness that cancer patients often come to at the end, and the shocking challenge to us all that we must give up everything that has really mattered to our earthly egos.

Yet the final line is an affirmation of hope. It seems that the writer, in giving a variant spelling for the last word 'born(e)', wanted the pun to convey both a glorious new birth beyond death and the comfort of knowing that we will be carried to that country, just as a boat takes pilgrims to the island of the saints, across a threatening sea.

Lights Out

I have come to the borders of sleep,
The unfathomable deep
Forest, where all must lose
Their way, however straight
Or winding, soon or late;
They can not choose.

Many a road and track
That since the dawn's first crack
Up to the forest brink
Deceived the travellers,
Suddenly now blurs,
And in they sink.

Here love ends –
Despair, ambition ends;
All pleasure and all trouble,
Although most sweet or bitter,
Here ends, in sleep that is sweeter
Than tasks most noble.

There is not any book
Or face of dearest look
That I would not turn from now
To go into the unknown
I must enter, and leave, alone,
I know not how.

The tall forest towers:
Its cloudy foliage lowers
Ahead, shelf above shelf:
Its silence I hear and obey
That I may lose my way
And myself.

Edward Thomas

Edward Thomas is remembered as one of the astonishing company
of poets who flourished as writers during the First World War, and
sadly died during active service. He was 37 when he enlisted in 1915,

even though as a married man with children he could have avoided doing so. He had only recently started writing poetry, although he was already a distinguished literary critic. He was inspired to do so by a new friend, Robert Frost, an American writer who lived in England from 1912 until 1915, when he returned to America. Although encouraged as a poet by his friend, Thomas took very seriously Frost's poem 'The Road not Taken' as a critique of his own tendency to melancholy and indecision, and it seems to have been the final straw that prompted him to enlist in the army.

'Lights Out' seems to me to be a meditation on foreseeing one's own death by a young man in good health, which is nevertheless very different from the poems in the 'Fears and fantasies' section of this book. Given the shocking statistics about survival rates of those fighting on the Western Front, there is a genuine realism in supposing that death was imminent. Nevertheless, the poem does not mention the war explicitly; it explores the speaker's inward attitude towards the inevitable prospect of death, and as such the text could be the words of anyone facing death soon, who has somehow reached a position of acceptance of it.

'Lights Out' as a title hints at army discipline, when it is decreed that it is time for sleep. But it also has other possible resonances, including the suggestion that signs of life or hope have been extinguished, or that darkness is falling in both the real and the metaphorical sense, and one is entering the unknown. Sleep itself, of course, is traditionally seen as an image or foretaste of death: it comes inevitably and often unbidden; we nevertheless have to surrender to it, and in it we lose our normal waking selves. This moment of letting ourselves fall asleep is announced from the start – but the reader is aware that this poem is not simply about going to bed: 'I have come to the borders of sleep'. Somehow the word 'borders' (with the menace implied in a context of deadly conflict zones) makes it clear that death is involved.

The poem has a regular rhyme scheme (AABCCB) and short lines, but the rhythm is somewhat irregular and the poet makes use of *enjambement* (carrying on the pulse of a line over the line ending so that you need to keep reading for the sense), which disrupts any sense of 'settling' at the end of a line. In the first stanza this technique has the effect of emphasizing the continuous forward movement into the unknown, which cannot be postponed: 'The unfathomable deep/ Forest, where all must lose/ Their way'.

The second stanza takes up the theme of roads, tracks and travelling – surely tediously and endlessly part of the military life at this time, but perhaps also recalling the 'road less travelled by' of Frost's poem and the long country walks the two writers had shared. For Thomas the image may have been painfully one about major and life-changing decisions. The image is of a track that during all the daylight hours of life seemed straightforward to follow, but this, the poem suggests, 'Deceived the travellers', since now it 'blurs' and sinks into a forest where the way ahead cannot be seen. Those who know they are approaching their death, perhaps because of illness or infirmity, often see themselves as being on a path that gradually becomes less defined, and involves going forward to somewhere quite uncertain, unaccompanied by loved ones (who, just because they are not dying right now, are not on that path with them).

The third stanza announces indeed that 'Here love ends'; but it goes on to list other things, and we see that this is not a depressive or gloomy complaint, but a matter-of-fact statement of the necessary way things are. The dying are inescapably on their own, but it is also true that they are moving beyond their involvement in hardship as well as joy: despair, trouble and bitterness fall away, as well as ambition, pleasure and all that is sweet. Instead, the narrator affirms, there is a 'sleep that is sweeter/ Than tasks most noble'. It is interesting that the sense of duty that brought the soldier to this encounter with death itself ebbs away. The fourth stanza is extraordinary because it seems to affirm even the turning away from loved ones and friends; it is a kind of choosing to 'go into the unknown', rather than fighting against the possibility. It is observably costly and sometimes terribly hard for the dying person to let go and leave loved ones at the point of death. There is often a fear of letting them down by ceasing to 'fight' any more. Yet it is necessary, and perhaps the most serene deaths happen when the dying person does, in a sense, turn away.

In the last stanza, we are left looking at the 'tall forest', as if very close to. It 'towers' and its foliage 'lowers', the trees thickening and building upon one another in looming ranks, 'shelf above shelf'. The poem stops just before the forest of death is actually entered. In the northern European psyche the image of the dark forest is a powerful one, suggesting a mysterious place where one may get lost and where all the rules are different. To step into this forest alone is an act of great courage, but may open up a whole unimaginable adventure.

The poet uses the language of military discipline for his response 'I hear and obey'. Yet what he obeys is not a barked command from a sergeant major, but 'Its silence'. And the obedient response is not about action but about loss of direction, loss of self. What will come next is left completely unknown. But there is a gentle and determined resolve in this poem that is like the resolve we see on the faces of those who are making a good death.

Do not go gentle into that good night

Do not go gentle into that good night,
Old age should burn and rave at close of day;
Rage, rage against the dying of the light.

Though wise men at their end know dark is right,
Because their words had forked no lightning they
Do not go gentle into that good night.

Good men, the last wave by, crying how bright
Their frail deeds might have danced in a green bay,
Rage, rage against the dying of the light.

Wild men who caught and sang the sun in flight,
And learn, too late, they grieved it on its way,
Do not go gentle into that good night.

Grave men, near death, who see with blinding sight
Blind eyes could blaze like meteors and be gay,
Rage, rage against the dying of the light.

And you, my father, there on the sad height,
Curse, bless, me now with your fierce tears, I pray.
Do not go gentle into that good night.
Rage, rage against the dying of the light.

Dylan Thomas

The last two poems in this section focus not on the inward thoughts of the dying but on the feelings and reflections of those who are beside them and watching them as they approach death. 'Do not go gentle into that good night' is perhaps Dylan Thomas' most famous poem; it has been set to music and has provided material for reflection for several generations of readers. It seems to have an appeal to modern sensibility, by reversing the traditional expectation that serenity, acceptance and a peaceful conscience are what constitute the right approach to a good death. The energetic refusal of the inevitable, even 'rage', are what the poet seems to be recommending.

Thomas' father David was the senior English master at Swansea Grammar, and used to read Shakespeare to the young Dylan at bedtime, bathing him in wonderful creative language long before he could understand most of it. But he had wished to be a poet, and has been described (by Thomas' wife Caitlin) as unhappy: 'He was unhappy with his life. It was exactly the kind of life he had hoped not to have.' This is rather what the narrator of the poem seems to believe about his father, though it is noticeable that the whole burden of the poem is that it is an effort to galvanize someone who seems, to the narrator, to be too 'gentle' about dying, not furious or resistant enough. (It is not surprising that those who have to do with palliative care, assisting the dying to live well in the moment and to die without distress, do not tend to approve of what this poem recommends – and I must say I hope no one reads it to me on my deathbed.)

But was the person to whom this poem is addressed actually dying? Many commentators assume that he was. But the poem was first published in a journal in 1951, and David Thomas did not die until the end of 1952 (tragically followed by the death of his son only a few months later, at the age of 39). It seems likely that Dylan Thomas' writing of this poem was prompted by a period of illness in his father, and that Thomas at the time believed his father was dying. However, this was clearly not the case, and it does seem to me that the emotions of the poem belong firmly not in the figure of a clearly observed dying person but in the psyche of the narrator, who himself is struggling with the failure to achieve dramatic significance and influence in the world. It feels truthful because it chimes with the continuing ambitions and growing disappointments of middle age.

The poem is a masterpiece of form. It is a villanelle, a traditional form surrounded with huge constraints. Every line rhymes with another, but there are only two rhymes throughout. There are five three-line stanzas, in which the last line is like a refrain, which alternates every other verse. Finally there is a four-line stanza, where the two refrains are brought together like a rhyming couplet to conclude the poem. It is an extraordinary achievement to handle such a difficult form, which in lesser hands could easily become banal, for the exploration of such powerful feelings. The very tightness of the form implies that we are containing chaos here, which might otherwise burst forth.

As always, Thomas wrenches the grammar around. I remember first reading the poem as a punctilious teenager, and being outraged by the word 'gentle' (because it should have been an adverb, 'gently'). And yet it makes the reader hear the emphasis on the word. The narrator does not want his father to be a gentle person at all in this context; he wants him to go on being an energetic mentor. And immediately there is paradox. 'Into that good night' seems to recognize that death is, in spite of any protestations by the living, a good and not an evil kind of dark. And the phrase absolutely recalls bedtime. At the same time, this whole stanza is in the imperative; the speaker is telling his father off and begging him to 'rage'.

Given the difficulty of including so many repeated lines, the poem brilliantly introduces variation by making the four internal stanzas use the phrases 'do not go gentle' and 'rage, rage' in the indicative mood (this is what people do), only returning to the imperative (this is what I'm telling you to do) in the last verse again. So the different kinds of men (and I suspect he really did mean male people, given their obsessions) described in the four internal stanzas become a list of 'evidence' why the poet's exhortation should be heard. When we examine the evidence, paradox returns. 'Wise' men apparently do 'know dark is right'; the night is 'good' – and yet they appear to wish their words had forked some lightning. The image is of dramatic and fearsome impact, lighting up the night sky. However, we have to admit that lightning is quintessentially a very temporary phenomenon. With the 'good' men, the image changes to a coastal one, very familiar to Thomas. Yet anyone living near the sea knows how changeable the weather is, and how sunlight and bobbing boats in a 'green bay' can switch to grey destructive waves that threaten life. 'Wild men' seems to refer to poets, who 'caught and sang the sun in flight' – and yet the overriding mood is not of deathless verses but the desperately fast passing of time itself. The verse about 'Grave men' (pun no doubt intended) is hard to interpret, but is stuffed with images of blindness, and insight that arrives just much too late in life. The narrator may be adjuring his father to be like these men, yet all their efforts seem to be in vain. Meteors, like lightning, represent a highly temporary flash of light.

Only in the very last verse does the narrator explicitly address his father. He asks for a paradoxical curse-cum-blessing; he wants him to swear and rage, but believes this will be a blessing for him – though surely the poet is galvanizing himself here, and not his father. And the 'fierce tears' (a phrase spoken slowly and very distinctly in the famous BBC recording performed by Dylan Thomas himself) are surely the poet's own.

Reading Aloud to My Father

I chose the book haphazard
from the shelf, but with Nabokov's first
sentence I knew it wasn't the thing
to read to a dying man:
The cradle rocks above an abyss, it began,
and common sense tells us that our existence
is but a brief crack of light
between two eternities of darkness.

The words disturbed both of us immediately,
and I stopped. With music it was the same –
Chopin's Piano Concerto – he asked me
to turn it off. He ceased eating, and drank
little, while the tumors briskly appropriated
what was left of him.

But to return to the rocking cradle. I think
Nabokov had it wrong. This is the abyss.
That's why babies howl at birth,
and why the dying so often reach
for something only they can apprehend.

At the end they don't want their hands
to be under the covers, and if you should put
your hand on theirs in a tentative gesture
of solidarity, they'll pull the hand free;
and you must honor that desire,
and let them pull it free.

Jane Kenyon

Jane Kenyon was a New England poet living on a rural farm, and she seems to have been both highly observant of the details of life and given to rather intellectual reading matter, which she sometimes boldly incorporates within her deceptively simple, brief poems. This poem comes over as a reflective memory about watching at her father's deathbed, and what she observes and reports convinces us that she really did witness a death. This is because of the element of surprise about the behaviour of the dying man, and her insight that her own needs and expectations about the event are not the most important thing.

The poem starts straight in, in a conversational way: 'I chose the book haphazard/ from the shelf', and by her instantly stated regret conveys to us that we are in the presence of the dying – someone she was about to read to out loud, as the title announces. Her random choice of book introduces the concept that there may be something appropriate to read to a dying man, even though Nabokov is probably not it. So we are aware not only of the psyche of the dying, but the speculation of the living woman about how she is supposed to meet the requirements of this unique moment, the death of her father. Perhaps many of us do not give a lot of thought to what might be helpful to someone on their deathbed; instead, we may very occasionally find ourselves there, but totally without resources to offer or words to say.

Appropriate or not, the narrator gives us the famous opening words, about the cradle rocking over an abyss, and human existence as a crack of light between two eternities of darkness. This, apparently, is 'common sense'; and indeed, for much of the post-Christian modern world, it has been accepted as such for perhaps a hundred years. There are very many churchgoers who, if pressed, might admit that it comes close to what they also believe, namely that we all come from the dark and are all headed towards the dark. Not that such a conviction (which at least removes the fear of hell) necessarily saves us from despair (see Philip Larkin's 'Aubade', p. 42). The image of the rocking cradle indeed awakens feelings that go well beyond common sense. The fragility of human existence is depicted as frightening and pitiful.

The second stanza notes how disturbing the thought was to both the dying man and his daughter who was keeping vigil. She reports trying music, which he similarly rejected. The narrator doesn't explain what was wrong with Chopin's Piano Concerto; perhaps it was the haunting sadness and poignancy of the music. This whole stanza has a very matter-of-fact feel, in which that heart-rending music is out of place. Her father wants the music turned off; he has stopped eating; he hardly drinks; and his tumours 'briskly appropriated/ what was left of him'. These lines remind us of the physical processes that are bringing about death, and will do so whatever deep or emotional meanings the human beings involved invest it with. But they also point out the agency and determination of the dying person to make choices and cooperate with what is happening.

In the third verse, the narrator stands back and returns to the 'rocking cradle', arguing that (along with most of the Western world) 'Nabokov had it wrong. This is the abyss'. This rather huge thought is not dwelt on particularly, but is just evidenced by the 'howl' of the newborn, who leave a place of security and peace for a cold, empty world, and the sense that the dying are reaching out for something only they can begin to grasp.

Finally, there is a detailed observation that the narrator attributes not just to her dying father but to all at the end. She starts to generalize and say that 'they' don't want their hands held: 'they'll pull the hand free'. Whether this is true of all who are at the point of death, it is observably true for some people, and it is a very counter-intuitive observation for those loved ones who sit beside the bed. We want to hold the hand of the departing, and it is hard to believe that they don't wish for this, if they still know who we are. But there is here a very strong contrast with Dylan Thomas' poem (p. 78). Rather than being concerned with what kind of blessing her father is leaving for her, she distances herself from her own needs to engage in a loving gesture, and stresses the need to honour the freedom of the dying, as they turn away in order to enter the space that is unknown to us, but which they alone may apprehend.

IMMEDIATE GRIEF

Sad Music

We fall to the earth like leaves
Lives as brief as footprints in snow
No words express the grief we feel
I feel I cannot let her go.

For she is everywhere.
Walking on the windswept beach
Talking in the sunlit square.
Next to me in the car
I see her sitting there.

At night she dreams me
and in the morning the sun does not rise.
My life is as thin as the wind
And I am done with counting stars.

She is gone   she is gone.
I am her sad music, and I play on, and on, and on.

Roger McGough

The poems in this section focus on the immediate aftermath of a death. Whatever the dying process has been like – long drawn out or sudden; serene or fearful; surrounded with love or ambivalence – and whatever are the religious beliefs of those who survive, the fact of death is a non-negotiable reality that ends something finally, and forever interrupts the conversation that used to exist. Bereaved people, even if they have beliefs that may be apparently consoling in the face of death, are in no way spared the often confusing sequence of feelings and responses that all humans are subject to when someone they love dies. Sometimes, religious people have the further blow that they feel unable to access any sense of the love of God, or indeed of any meaning or comfort at all in the face of death's unanswerable power.

One of the first reactions may be wordlessness, numbness and a sensation that one's own body has become insubstantial, and this brief poem by Roger McGough conveys some of this reaction. The language is immensely simple and undramatic, almost as if every word has been got out singly, with great pain attached. There is no need for the speaker to emphasize anything or try to explain it in a clever way; it is the enormity of the fact of death that dominates the poem.

It begins with a phrase that is quite conventional as an idea, that of autumn leaves that 'fall to the earth', but the generalization soon focuses on the particular death that this poem announces. There is a bitter parallel made with the assonance of 'leaves' and 'lives' between the first and second lines, and the image of transient footprints in snow underlines the poignantly temporary nature of human life. Again, there is something very conventional about the complaint about a loss of words ('No words express the grief we feel'); it is one of the most commonplace of helpless remarks made to the bereaved around their loss. The speaker here does not try to find variations on this continuously rediscovered truth about grief. But then he makes the transitions, on the hinge of the line, between general truth and agonized personal cry: 'the grief we feel/ I feel I cannot let her go'.

The second stanza picks up another widely experienced phenomenon of early grief, namely that the dead beloved is 'everywhere'. He mentions situations that no doubt recall actual, perhaps repeated memories: the windswept beach, the sunlit square, her place in the car. It could be that the speaker is experiencing the sensation of actually seeing this woman who is dead, inhabiting those familiar locations as if she were alive, or perhaps these are vivid memories that are crowding in and seeming more real just now than the corpse (which is not described or focused on at all). The poem does not say what the emotional tone of these memories is, except by implication through the title of the poem, 'Sad Music'. The recounting of visual memories that are clearly important and probably happy is sufficient to underline the experience of massive loss. How is it possible that this crucially important and loved person simply is not there, where she should be?

The third stanza looks at the speaker himself more closely. Sleep is profoundly disturbed by grief; commonly, a bereaved person finds it hard to stay asleep or to surrender to it in the first place, and dreams can be odd. He conveys some of this weirdness by reversing what we expect to hear: 'At night she dreams me'. His own agency and sense of selfhood is immersed in hers, although he is here and she is not. The sadness imprints itself on the natural world: 'in the morning the sun does not rise'. It does, of course, but not within the psyche of the profoundly sad. The next line conveys brilliantly that sensation of bodily insubstantiality that can afflict someone who is just coming to terms with a death – as if the wind could blow straight through you (this is why you may forget to eat). And the last line, 'I am done with counting stars', refers to the austere comfort that may be derived by the grief-stricken from gazing at a starry sky, either because it puts your suffering in perspective or because thinking of the loved one as a star is helpful. The speaker seems to be finally rejecting this search for comfort, having tried it and failed to be consoled.

The final two lines bluntly accept the terrible reality: 'She is gone she is gone'. This bleak repetition of the fact is rhymed with a statement about the condition of the mourner: 'I am her sad music, and I play on, and on, and on'. It is a brilliant twist. Just as the dead woman dreams the speaker, so he becomes her music, unable to cease playing the tune of her continued life within him. And how true it is that those in grief find that they wish to talk endlessly of their beloved, however painful it is to do so, however bored they are with their pain, and however unable their friends may be to engage in that conversation yet again.

Dirge Without Music

I am not resigned to the shutting away of loving hearts in the hard
    ground.
So it is, and so it will be, for so it has been, time out of mind:
Into the darkness they go, the wise and the lovely. Crowned
With lilies and with laurel they go; but I am not resigned.

Lovers and thinkers, into the earth with you.
Be one with the dull, the indiscriminate dust.
A fragment of what you felt, of what you knew,
A formula, a phrase remains, – but the best is lost.

The answers quick and keen, the honest look, the laughter, the
    love, –
They are gone. They are gone to feed the roses. Elegant and curled
Is the blossom. Fragrant is the blossom. I know. But I do not
    approve.
More precious was the light in your eyes than all the roses in the
    world.

Down, down, down into the darkness of the grave
Gently they go, the beautiful, the tender, the kind;
Quietly they go, the intelligent, the witty, the brave.
I know. But I do not approve. And I am not resigned.

Edna St Vincent Millay

Edna St Vincent Millay was an American poet of the early twentieth
century who lived a bohemian life in New York's Greenwich village,
and maintained her interest in producing lyrical, expressive poetry
at a time when the mainstream was tending to favour esoteric, intel-
lectual and rather distanced poetry that was hard to understand. An
activist and a feminist, and famous for engaging in many love affairs
with both men and women, she nevertheless seems to have reserved
her deepest commitment for her writing. Many people dealing with
early grief may find that this poem articulates exactly their struggle
to accept the undeniable fact of the death of their loved one, while
needing to retain their profound sense of outrage that people should
have to die at all.

    The poem first evokes and then denies what it claims to be, for
a 'dirge' is precisely a funeral song, sung to lament, celebrate and

protect the dead (see 'Fidele's Dirge', p. 15). This poem does indeed go on to celebrate the dead, but it also proclaims an undefeated resistance to the whole notion that funerals should be necessary. Some kind of acceptance of death is expressed, but the speaker is damned if she is going to offer death the kind of resignation that is implied by making a song of her poem. This sense of existing simultaneously within two firmly incompatible tracks of reality is characteristic of how we as sentient human beings experience our own imminent deaths or the immediate deaths of others close to us. Something that is an undeniable fact is also an outrage against reality and meaning.

The poem is constructed with very long lines that lend themselves to determined announcements (even if these fly in the face of the facts), and the simple ABAB rhyme scheme hammers these home, even if they cannot be sustained as true. All the actual evidence and argument within the poem, sadly, affirms that people do die, even if they are wise, lovely, honest, cheerful or kind, but the speaker is resolved to set her sheer disapproval against the inexorable truth of human mortality. The very first line is magisterial and absurd simultaneously, and thus achieves an extraordinary poignancy: 'I am not resigned to the shutting away of loving hearts in the hard ground'.

The speaker is clearly attending or recalling a burial, and everything in her wants to shriek that this necessity is simply unacceptable. The process is described as if it is brutal and cruel, as it would be if someone were still alive. Nevertheless the speaker immediately admits that 'So it is, and so it will be, for so it has been' – past, present and future all bear witness to the truth that no one is exempt, and good behaviour does not enable us to evade death: 'Into the darkness they go, the wise and the lovely'. Even if the dead are honoured, 'Crowned/ With lilies and with laurel', the speaker wants to assert, echoing the opening of the poem, 'but I am not resigned'. (It is interesting to compare the sentiment with Rupert Brooke's 'The Hill', p. 31.)

The second stanza almost seems to adopt the perspective of death itself, who apparently chivvies everyone, whether passionate and thoughtful or quite otherwise, 'into the earth with you', almost as if the value of people's individual lives is simply thrown away into dull 'indiscriminate dust'. Distinctions, achievements, identity, feelings are all, it seems, turned into rubbish, with only fragments of memory remaining – 'A formula, a phrase'. It is a depressing thought, and not surprising that the speaker rebels against it.

However, the next stanza seems to reclaim some strong and positive memories from this dust heap: 'The answers quick and keen, the honest look, the laughter, the love'. You have the sense that the speaker is now recalling an actual person, not generalizing about humanity. But the vivid reactions and vital engagement in the relationship with the speaker is precisely what has been lost, and so the poem collapses into the despair of the previous verse, even employing a traditionally dismissive phrase about the passing of life: 'They are gone to feed the roses'. But then that very phrase is taken up and developed in a lyrical way, as if the style and beauty of the one who died has in fact emerged again in the roses that grow from her dust. Half-ironically, the speaker uses short, rather poetic phrases, with the adjectives preceding the noun: 'Elegant and curled/ Is the blossom. Fragrant is the blossom'. And once again the paradox, the double track of reality, is affirmed: 'I know. But I do not approve'. The clipped phrases and the language of approval could almost come from a society hostess who is pontificating in a tight-lipped way about some aspect of fashion or morality – this is heavy with irony not just because it is about death but because the poet was famous for her defiance of convention. But the stanza ends with the only line that is addressed directly to the beloved dead, and it claims the more power because it is surrounded with generalized denial: 'More precious was the light in your eyes than all the roses in the world'.

The last verse really feels like a passionate dirge, with its frequent repetitions and a new sense of gentleness that succeeds the personal statement of love and loss. Here, the generalizations about all the glorious people who cannot avoid going down 'into the darkness of the grave' seem to create a community of the dead, and briefly it seems that the speaker has been able to feel more accepting about death's inevitability because she could speak her heart. But then it ends once more with the clipped phrases of fierce, furious rebellion against reality. Grief takes huge, repeated work, which includes sheer rage; and acceptance of death takes time.

Death of a Poet

Suddenly his mouth filled with sand.
His tractor of blood stopped thumping.
He held five icicles in each hand.
His heart packed up jumping.

His face turned the colour of something forgotten in the larder.
His thirty-two teeth were expelled on the kitchen floor.
His muscles, at long last, got considerably harder.
He felt younger than he had for some time before.

Four heroes, steady as wrestlers, each carried him on a shoulder
Into a great grey church laid out like a brain.
An iron bowl sent out stiff rays of chrysanthemums. It grew colder.
The sun, as expected, failed to break through the pane.

The parson boomed like a dockyard gun at a christening.
Somebody read from the bible. It seemed hours.
I got the feeling you were curled up inside the box, listening.
There was the thud of hymn-books, the stench of flowers.

I remembered hearing your voice on a bloody foment
Of Atlantic waters. The words burned clear as a flare.
Life begins, you said, *as of this moment*.
A bird flew down out of the hurling air.

Over the church a bell broke like a wave upended.
The hearse left for winter with a lingering hiss.
I looked in the wet sky for a sign, but no bird descended.
I went across the road to the pub; wrote this.

Charles Causley

Charles Causley, a Cornish poet of the twentieth century, was a
master of rhyme and often wrote verses that had the feel of ballads:
that is, having a deceptive simplicity and 'sing-song' rhythm, but
unfolding a poignant narrative and often packing a mighty punch at
the end of lines. In his approach, he stood outside the mainstream of
modernist poets and was in that sense 'unfashionable', yet his poetry
has always been popular for its accessibility and passion.

This poem, which describes the death and funeral of a friend
known to the speaker in earlier years as a fellow mariner in the Royal

Navy in the Second World War, is remarkable for its bluntness about death's reality. Wartime experience was central to Causley's development as a writer. He later remarked, 'I think I became a working poet the day I joined the destroyer *Eclipse* at Scapa Flow in August, 1940.' The poem is remarkable for its sheer anger within the speaker's response to the funeral. Anger is often a powerful and shocking dimension of the experience of grief, and can take mourners by surprise, especially those with religious faith, who may assume that they ought not to feel such an ugly emotion, especially if it is directed at God. While God is not directly mentioned here, Causley was a Christian writer, and the rage experienced during the funeral service has the feel to me of 'insider' critique.

The first stanza takes us directly into the sudden moment of death, which is presumably a heart attack or stroke. From the details in the second verse, we assume that this has taken place in a domestic kitchen, but the opening of the poem is full of arresting images that focus on the body, describing it in ways that remove its agency and humanity. The mouth that fills with sand does so because the body has collapsed on the floor; we do not even see the fall, it is so quick. His circulation is like a machine that has just cut out like a faulty tractor. The connections have 'packed up jumping'. His fingers are not fingers any more but 'icicles'; the blood is simply not there any more. The lines in this first stanza are short and stark, like the announcement of very sudden death.

The second stanza continues the theme, and adds some details that have an element of humour in them: the dramatic change of complexion, 'the colour of something forgotten in the larder'; his false teeth that shoot out of his mouth across the floor; the muscles that harden with rigor mortis, in a grim parody of the hard, fit body that he had when he was a younger man. It may seem strange that the speaker introduces humour into this terrible moment, but it is noticeable that 'gallows humour' around death and dying arises naturally among those who are dealing with the immediate physical reality. It is only those who are quite distant who can maintain a uniform conventional solemnity about what it means to die and how one copes with death.

The narrative proceeds to the man's funeral. The men who are carrying the coffin, perhaps old naval comrades, are described as 'heroes, steady as wrestlers', which conveys both the weight of the coffin and that committed, concentrated way that pall bearers move. The task is onerous because they must stay in step, because it is the focus of the ceremony at that moment, and perhaps because they are in grief. The extraordinary comparison of the layout of the church to that of a 'brain' presumably refers to the way that a central aisle divides one side of the church from the other, like the twin hemispheres of the brain. But it also reminds us of the harsh fact of death, as if we were witnessing a post mortem. The funeral flower arrangement is similarly cold and bleak, with its 'stiff rays of chrysanthemums'. And the weak winter sun is described as failing to penetrate the windows. A sense of deep chill frequently surrounds those in deep grief.

The conduct of the funeral is alienating to the speaker of the poem, who is completely disengaged from what is going on. The parson's voice booms like gunfire at a dockyard 'christening' – but this is a death, not the launch of a heroic ship. Short half-lines emphasize the irrelevance and tedium of the experience: 'Somebody read from the bible. It seemed hours.' The speaker finds himself imagining the dead person somehow cosily present and listening ironically; but his fantasy is interrupted by the sounds and smells of the church. These are described as if they are hostile, not solemn or comforting: 'There was the thud of hymn-books, the stench of flowers'. It may be that grief lends an unusual sensitivity to sense impressions; but certainly, the person describing the funeral like this is deeply angry.

The penultimate verse lifts the speaker out of the unsatisfactory present into a vivid memory of an earlier time. Though full of danger and hardship (it was 'a bloody foment/ Of Atlantic waters'), it is remembered for the voice of the man who has died, fully inhabiting his exultation in his young life and strength. The title of the poem suggests that this friend was himself a poet, perhaps also having his gift honed in the comradeship of war. The speaker recalls how, in the midst of battle, 'A bird flew down out of the hurling air'. This detail reminds us of a hugely significant moment in the Bible, when after the baptism of Jesus the voice of God is heard from the sky and it seems as if the spirit of God is descending like a dove over his head (Mark 1.10).

The final verse returns to the actual church, where the funeral has ended and there is a bell tolling overhead that seems to break with sound 'like a wave upended', as if we are still in violent Atlantic waters.

The last three lines continue the savage disappointment inherent in the rest of the funeral: there is no sign in the sky to crown this moment; no bird descends (where is the so-called comfort of the Holy Spirit at a time like this?); there is nothing to do but repair to the pub and scrawl an angry poem. Throughout these lines the thick use of sibilants reinforces our sense of a hostile parade: the 'lingering hiss' of the hearse; the 'wet sky' with no 'sign', the contempt in that final word 'this'. Apart from that one vivid memory, the poet allows us no relief.

Wish

But what if, in the clammy soil, her limbs
grew warmer, shifted, stirred, kicked off
the covering of earth, the drowsing corms,
the sly worms, what if her arms reached out
to grab the stone, the grooves of her dates
under her thumb, and pulled her up? I wish.
Her bare feet walk along the gravel path
between the graves, her shroud like washing
blown onto the grass, the petals of her wreath
kissed for a bride. Nobody died. Nobody
wept. Nobody slept who couldn't be woken
by the light. If I can only push open this heavy door
she'll be standing there in the sun, dirty, tired,
wondering why do I shout, why do I run.

Carol Ann Duffy

One of the features of early grief is a tendency to experience delusions, as the shocked mind of the bereaved seeks to come to terms with the reality of death and the total, final interruption that it causes within a relationship of love. Either in the waking or the sleeping consciousness, it is common to experience fantasies, or episodes that feel like reality and not fantasy, in which the deceased person returns from the dead, or reveals that it is all a mistake and they never actually died at all, or is simply 'there' in an uncomplicated way that takes no account of the event of death. There seems to be in the human psyche an implicit sense of outrage at the fact of a death, even though we know in principle that it happens to us all, and even though we may have witnessed the moment of death for this person, or participated in the funeral at which the body was either buried or relinquished for cremation. One of the main reasons for the rituals surrounding a death is to enable those for whom the death matters to gather together and name the reality that this death has happened – as unacceptable or as meaningless as that fact may be to them. For those closest to the person, the fact has to be faced repeatedly, and accepted as non-negotiable, again and again before the psyche is able to regard a world without this person in it as the 'new normal'.

This poem by Carol Ann Duffy explores this process. It is a sonnet, but unlike more traditional sonnets, there are no end rhymes. The way the poet uses this form, it is more like a Shakespearean sonnet than a Petrarchan one: there is no division of thought into the first eight lines (the octet) and then the answering sestet. The thought runs through the whole poem and comes to a climax in the last two lines. The thought is about entertaining the possibility that the very recent death of a beloved woman (a partner? her mother?) is not, in fact, real. Brilliantly, the poem begins as it were in the middle of a sentence, 'But what if'. At this point, the event of her death is not explicitly mentioned, because it is simply the huge reality against which the speaker is opposing her passionate desire that it should not be true. The process of burial (which has clearly happened) is also not mentioned; we simply begin with the observation of 'the clammy soil', in which, it is imagined, the woman who has been buried there begins to move. 'Clammy' suggests soil that has recently been disturbed and handled, even touched with bare skin that can feel how cool and damp and sticky it is. And so we appear to be in the presence of a grave, where the earth has only recently been filled in.

Then the imagination creates a mental picture of this buried woman first growing warmer (so there is an admission that she was first of all cold), and then shifting, stirring and finally kicking off 'the covering of earth' exactly as if she had just been sound asleep in bed and was in the process of waking up and throwing off the bed covering prior to getting up. You have the sense that the speaker in this poem has seen her beloved wake from sleep many times and this is an expected and normal occurrence. Yet the poem stays with the scene of the graveyard, seeing this process of 'getting up' (or indeed, rising like Lazarus from the tomb in John 11, or like the people in paintings by Stanley Spencer rising from their ordinary English graves on resurrection day) very much from the perspective of the woman who has died. She notices what you would presumably only notice from the underneath – 'the drowsing corms,/ the sly worms'. And then, in order to emerge back into the world, there is an extraordinary description of how her arms reach up, grab the tombstone and heave her body up and out of the grave. The detail that she feels 'the grooves of her dates/ under her thumb' as she does so is very telling. It insists upon the perspective of the once dead woman (only she would notice such a thing); as with the 'clammy soil' it highlights the importance of touch as evidence of life; and at the same time it brings together the two conflicting tracks of reality that is the lived experience of the mourner. The 'dates' on the tombstone make it clear that the death has happened and there is a reliable end date for the story of this woman's life. But the fact that her thumbs can feel the grooves proposes that she is in fact alive. This long question, which has taken six lines to complete, is answered by the terse 'I wish'. The speaker does acknowledge that this is a wish and not what is the case.

But then the fantasy plays on, counteracting that acknowledgement once more. The woman is up and out, and her bare feet are on the gravel path, her shroud 'like washing/ blown onto the grass'. Notice how the image takes a concept as gloomy and final as a shroud and normalizes it back to something as unthreatening as washing that has been hung outside and has been blown down on to the lawn. The 'petals of her wreath', which were presumably buried in the coffin with her, have become something connected with weddings and celebrations instead. The poem then moves into a series of very short, blunt assertions with 'Nobody', which totally deny what has happened. Interestingly, rhymes like echoes are suddenly introduced: 'kissed for a bride. Nobody died. Nobody/ wept. Nobody slept who couldn't be woken'.

The speaker is now fully into the fantasy conviction that there is something she could do – 'If I can only push open this heavy door' – which would make the death of her beloved no longer true. This stage of grief is often called 'bargaining', the implicit belief (however irrational) that the mourner can affect the facts of death by means of some sort of struggle, or by behaving well, or even by engaging in 'grief work' properly. It feels as if one can potentially change the unacceptable situation by making the effort, or getting some strategy right. After all, this is normally the case in most other dilemmas that life presents us with. In this case, the 'heavy door' the speaker imagines is rather like the heavy tombstone that the dead person is imagined to have hauled herself up by.

But then the final two lines bring everything together: the wish that she be alive; the fantasy that she has arisen from her grave; and the (so far unmentioned) truth that such a vision would in fact be terrifying, because there is also a part of the mourner's psyche that knows that this is not normal. The woman is standing there, not as if she has never died, but as if she has, with considerable exertion, got out of her grave. However, she seems to be greeting her beloved as if her appearance is not odd. She is 'wondering why do I shout, why do I run'. The poet does not tell us which way the speaker is running; is it towards the woman who has died, or is it away from her, because the return of the dead, however longed for, would actually be horrifying? I think the poem brilliantly conveys both the power of wish fulfilment and the mind's implicit recognition that this is precisely what it is, and the task of grief is to gradually lay it down.

A Dirge

Why were you born when the snow was falling?
You should have come to the cuckoo's calling,
Or when grapes are green in the cluster,
Or at least when lithe swallows muster
  For their far off flying
  From summer dying.

Why did you die when the lambs were cropping?
You should have died at the apples' dropping,
When the grasshopper comes to trouble,
And the wheat-fields are sodden stubble,
  And all winds go sighing
  For sweet things dying.

Christina Rossetti

This intense, brief poem, which sounds like a song in the minor key, manages to be deeply poignant while remaining quite enigmatic about what kind of death this 'dirge' is actually addressing. There are vivid and precise images in the poem, but because we do not have more than a hint of the circumstances around the death, these images from the natural world have the effect of suggesting a kind of painful melancholy that is inherent in the nature of creation, which is constantly witnessing to 'sweet things dying'. Without a single explicit reference to the speaker's (or should it be singer's?) feelings, there is a kind of skinlessness here that is suggestive of early grief, when the fact of death has been accepted but the bereaved person feels painfully exposed to a cosmos that speaks of death wherever she looks. Everything that lives, even newly born creatures, are, in the words of Dylan Thomas' poem (p. 4), 'green and dying'.

The impression of a minor key is conveyed by using end words in each line that have a 'falling' rhythm. The emphasis is on the first syllable of each word, with a softer, unemphasized second syllable that gives the impression that the line is falling away, just as creatures in the natural world seem to be moving towards death almost as soon as they are born.

The tone of the poem is set by the fact that it is constructed as questions, to which the singer makes her own reply – and the reply suggests that things ought to have happened differently from how they did. The one who died is addressed directly, but as if they have made a mistake, and the mistake is around the timing of their birth and their death. The question 'why' is inevitably around when someone dies, unreasonable though it may be, and the particular focus of this question in this poem is completely unreasonable. Seldom does anyone make a choice about the timing of their own death, and none of us can choose the moment of our birth. And what would it mean, to suggest that another season of the year would have been better as a time to die? And yet the questions, and the reproaches about timing, *sound* like the endless, circling questions of genuine grief, which do not always make sense but keep re-presenting themselves to the stricken mind and heart of the bereaved. Any death may feel 'out of time', but, of course, this is true of some deaths more than others.

Without being able to pin it down definitely, I wonder if what we have here is mourning for a baby, perhaps one that was born much too soon ('Why were you born when the snow was falling?/ You should have come to the cuckoo's calling'). But it is impossible to fix on this, as to take it literally involves positing very late winter snow (February?) and quite an early arrival of the cuckoo (April?), to allow enough gestation time for a child to have lived even briefly. And in any case, the stanza then continues with the greening of the grapes and the swallows' preparation to depart (August/September?). So instead of letting us settle on an actual moment of birth, we are presented with the speedy progress of the seasons, so that summer comes and is then gone before we have completed six short lines. What we have watched is 'summer dying', and the stanza ends with an image of planning to escape this, and what comes next. The 'lithe' swallows (notice how that single adjective stresses their lively resilience) are taking themselves 'far off' from the winter that already approaches. Unlike the speaker, who is unable to escape her grief.

The second stanza echoes the question of the first one, but this time asking about the season of death. The lambs 'cropping' could mean the time of the first birthing of the lambs – the first 'crop' of lambs (not very long after the winter snows). Or it could refer to the slightly larger lambs, which are out in the fields and have already started to crop the grass themselves, rather than suckling the ewes. Either meaning still suggests spring. A child might have been born during the snows of winter and not survived beyond springtime. There is something about this poem that suggests that very vulnerable period around a birth when it is not completely certain (even today, let alone in the Victorian period) that the child will thrive. As this stanza proceeds, it seems to make more sense to assert that death would have been more timely, or at least in keeping with what is happening in the rest of creation, if it had occurred when everything else is moving towards autumn: the dropping apples, the doomed grasshopper, the 'sodden stubble'. Even the winds of autumn could have become like weeping mourners, 'sighing/ For sweet things dying'.

And yet, of course, there is no good, right time for death. There is only a profound sadness deep down, and this poem captures that, without ever quite letting us settle on what it means.

The Unprofessionals

When the worst happens,
That uproots the future,
That you must live for every hour of your future,

They come,
Unorganized, inarticulate, unprofessional;

They come sheepishly, sit with you, holding hands,
From tea to tea, from Anadin to Valium,
Sleeping on put-you-ups, answering the phone,
Coming in shifts, spontaneously,

Talking sometimes,
About wallflowers, and fishing, and why
Dealing with Kleenex and kettles,
Doing the washing up and the shopping,

Like civilians in a shelter, under bombardment,
Holding hands and sitting it out
Through the immortality of all the seconds,
Until the blunting of time.

U. A. Fanthorpe

U. A. Fanthorpe was a Quaker poet who did not begin to write poetry until she was in her fifties, when she left her teaching post to take up a position as a receptionist in a psychiatric clinic. Her position gave her a perspective, placed between the authoritative medical staff and the vulnerable patients, that enabled her to notice the 'underside' of life, and her poetry often highlights the significance of those who normally go unnoticed.

This poem reflects not directly on the experience of grief but on the appearance and activity of those who often turn up at a time of bereavement and offer an instinctive, unobtrusive kind of practical support, even though they are neither trained nor obliged to do so through their professional role. They are not district nurses or undertakers or clergy; possibly they are not even long-term friends or family members, though they may be neighbours. In this poem they are given no name except the negative definition, 'The Unprofessionals'. As the poet describes what they do (by definition they do not draw attention to themselves), you realize that they provide an absolutely essential service for anyone enduring the first shock of bereavement.

We start right in, as if the 'worst' has just happened without warning. The word 'death' is not spoken here; we are in the normal conversational realm of homely circumlocution. But it is clear what is going on, because what has happened is the kind of thing that 'uproots the future,/ That you must live for every hour of your future'. The repetition circles around the idea of the future, as if the speaker is still piecing together what the cataclysmic event is going to mean in detail. Of course, the first thing that major bereavement does is to interrupt the narrative by which the survivor has constructed her life, where the imagined future had a similar reality to the memory of the shared past. Suddenly that has simply gone, and a new one must be laboriously constructed, starting right now, hour by hour.

The quiet arrival of the 'unprofessionals' is first announced in two lines standing alone. It is almost as if they are a natural phenomenon or a species of wildlife that will only be observed under certain conditions. They are described only in terms of what they are not, via three negative adjectives: 'unorganized, inarticulate, unprofessional'. It is the flip side of the common and distressing experience of many bereaved people, namely that some of those who might have been expected to be towers of strength in a crisis become strangely absent in the face of death, unable or unwilling to stay close.

By contrast, the 'unprofessionals' do arrive, though 'sheepishly', as if they feel they can claim no right to be there, or as if they do not suspect the value of their presence. There is nothing dramatic about their demeanour, and they simply do very ordinary things, like sitting, holding hands, making tea or fetching painkillers. Unbidden, they seem to look after themselves ('Sleeping on put-you-ups'), while also shielding the mourner from social demands ('answering the phone') and, without making a big deal of it, recognizing other 'unprofessionals' sufficiently to operate in shifts without having to devise a fixed plan that the bereaved person notices at all.

These are not people who demand meaningful conversations of the bereaved, or indeed any attention to their own needs and agenda. The conversation may be quite gentle and commonplace, while being willing to accommodate major, agonized questions in the midst of ordinary topics, which may be 'About wallflowers, and fishing, and why'. It is as if the unanswerable is allowed to be incorporated within the realms of normality, which indeed it must be if life is to go on and be endured. Tears may be accommodated and these people will hand out the Kleenex and make more tea. They do not let the drama of the event overwhelm everything, but ensure that basic matters like washing up and shopping continue even when the main sufferer cannot possibly cope with these. Thus life is maintained.

The poet calls up an image from her own childhood during the war to describe these unnamed folk who keep things going; she recalls the sudden, unasked-for connection between relative strangers cooped up in a bomb shelter when the siren goes. All are civilians 'under bombardment', recognizing their common vulnerability, taking turns to comfort those who specially need reassurance, 'Holding hands and sitting it out'. For sudden grief is like being under attack, and very exposed to danger that makes no sense in the moment, and could perhaps get worse. Human beings find that we need the practical, comforting, undemanding presence of each other in order to get through this terrifying, destabilizing reality.

The final lines again refer to the break-up of ordinary time. It is not just 'every hour' that has to be lived through in a new way, but 'the immortality of all the seconds', moment by moment. And in this first phase of grief there is no short cut to the construction of a new future. All that can be hoped for initially is 'the blunting of time', which is the stage that the unprofessionals are supporting the mourner to reach.

Common and Particular

I like these men and women who have to do with death,
Formal, gentle people whose job it is,
They mind their looks, they use words carefully.

I liked that woman in the sunny room
One after the other receiving such as me
Every working day. She asks the things she must

And thanks me for the answers. Then I don't mind
Entering your particulars in little boxes,
I like the feeling she has seen it all before,

There is a form, there is a way. But also
That no one come to speak up for a shade
Is like the last, I see she knows that too.

I'm glad there is a form to put your details in,
Your dates, the cause. Glad as I am of men
Who'll make a trestle of their strong embrace

And in a slot between two other slots
Do what they have to every working day:
Carry another weight for someone else.

It is common. You are particular.

David Constantine

In dealing with the aftermath of a death, survivors have to deal with
a range of professional people, and there is a significant amount of
administration work, which legally must be fulfilled within a limited
timeframe. These professionals are a quite different segment of the
working population from the medical and caring professions; they
do not arrive on the scene until death has actually taken place, and
they are workers most of us never encounter except under these
critical circumstances – undertakers, of course, but also, as explored
in this poem, registrars. Given that dealing with the details of death
is a key part of their job, it is common to find that the interview is
surprisingly gentle.

This poem by David Constantine is a kind of celebration of 'these
men and women who have to do with death', from the perspective

of one who has just had to go and register the death of someone important to him (just 'you' in the poem, as if it is so obvious who 'you' are that nothing more needs to be added as identification). The poem is addressed to the deceased, reflecting a common desire in the bereaved to continue conducting a comfortable everyday dialogue with the dead, just as they did during the life they lived together. The habits of companionship cannot easily be dropped just because death has interrupted the conversation, and the survivor is suddenly dealing with new encounters that the deceased might well have found interesting. In the tone of the poem, the expressions are almost like those one would expect from a curious child who is experiencing something for the first time and reporting on her impressions. There is simple repetition in the phrases, 'I like these men', 'I liked that woman', 'I like the feeling'; and the actual behaviour of the registrar is described in careful sequence, as if being seen for the first time and never really anticipated.

The poem proceeds with simple, three-line stanzas that do not rhyme or show any attempt to construct anything clever. It is as if just putting down the straightforward facts is enough of an effort. Overall, we have a sense that the speaker is perhaps shell-shocked, or just so vulnerable and sensitive from immediate grief that he is blessedly relieved to find that there are people who understand that he needs to be handled with great gentleness. He is noticing people's demeanour around him with a special clarity (and it is true, one does not forget how people respond around a death). Those whose job it is 'mind their looks, they use words carefully'.

The second stanza describes the registrar as she sits in a sunny room, and the speaker emphasizes, with a rather unusual and formal word order, what it is (from her perspective) she does every working day: 'One after the other receiving such as me'. You get the sense that he is having to work hard to stand outside his own acute crisis state, but that when he does he is able to appreciate that he is only one of an everyday procession of people who come before her, who are in exactly the same stage of grief as he is. The gentle politeness of the set interview questions and answers, which bridge two stanzas ('She asks the things she must/ And thanks me for the answers'), enables the speaker to feel comfortable about 'Entering your particulars in little boxes'.

The fact that the registrar has 'seen it all before', and that therefore 'There is a form, there is a way', has a certain real comfort in the speaker's situation. Those who are in early grief are often terribly disorientated and acutely lonely, and it is reassuring to know that there exists some kind of a roadmap out there, even if this is only evidenced by the existence of a legal form. Knowing that mortality is commonplace, and that there is a large community of the recently dead and the recently bereaved, is important. But the poem brings together this perception with the equally important need for the recognition of the utter individuality of this dead person and this suffering mourner: 'no one come to speak up for a shade/ Is like the last'.

For what actually makes up a death certificate acknowledges both the common and the particular: this is the common format and these are the things we need to know about the event and who is reporting it; these are the unique names and actual causes. The poem doesn't mention grief or pain – it doesn't need to – only the surprising gladness that is evoked by working through the process of registration. This is compared with the work of those other professionals around death, the undertakers. Their work of removing the body from the place of death and of carrying the coffin into the church or crematorium is described in a way that evokes not only their strength but their tenderness, as they 'make a trestle of their strong embrace'. Like the registrar, their interaction with the bereaved is commonplace; it happens 'in a slot between two other slots'. But they 'Carry another weight for someone else', and the implication is that this is not just a practical service but a pastoral one, which partly shoulders the burden for those in grief in an important psychological way. And because of this, what is common to humanity and yet profoundly about this individual death are both honoured: 'It is common. You are particular.'

The Minister

We're going to need the minister
to help this heavy body into the ground.

But he won't dig the hole;
others who are stronger and weaker will have to do that.
And he won't wipe his nose and his eyes;
others who are weaker and stronger will have to do that.
And he won't bake cakes or take care of the kids –
women's work. Anyway,
what would they do at a time like this
if they didn't do that?

No, we'll get the minister to come
and take care of the words.

He doesn't have to make them up,
he doesn't have to say them well,
he doesn't have to like them
so long as they agree to obey him.

We have to have the minister
so the words will know where to go.

Imagine them circling and circling
the confusing cemetery.
Imagine them roving the earth
without anywhere to rest.

Anne Stevenson

The previous poem, by David Constantine, explores the role of the
registrar and the undertakers in relation to the deceased person and
to the chief mourners. Here Anne Stevenson looks in an intriguing
way at the role of the minister who conducts the funeral (in this case,
a burial). It is written in a conversational tone, apparently by one of
the people who has the responsibility to organize the funeral, and it
is a potent blend of straightforwardly practical points and profoundly
symbolic speculation about what exactly it is that a minister is *for*
at this event. One of the most fascinating aspects of this speculation
is that it is expressed entirely without reference to any 'official' or
theological language about how a liturgy works when it is conducted

well (or poorly), but is purely couched in terms that an uninstructed but intuitive (perhaps even childlike) participant might use. And many who attend funerals may be unfamiliar with regular liturgy.

It starts where the previous poem ended, with a two-line announcement about the sheer weight of 'this heavy body' that needs to be helped into the ground. But because it starts 'We're going to need the minister', the reader is already alerted not just to the heavy physical presence of a corpse but to the need for something else to happen, which somehow makes it possible for a dead body to be rightly and honourably disposed of. A lifeless body does indeed feel much weightier to lift than a living person, who, however weak, cooperates with being lifted. But the weight involved is not just literal but psychic. A funeral effects a change that really moves things on in the life of the mourners, to a degree that is often surprising to them, and it is a shift that is about much more than just the completion of a necessary practical task.

The poem goes on to explore what it is that the minister does – initially by outlining what he doesn't do. In this poem it is assumed that a minister is male, and very conventional roles are assigned to the women mentioned. This may be to do with when the poem was written, or we may need to imagine that the community where this death has occurred holds conservative views about who rightly does what. There are several gendered tasks listed, and he will not be doing any of them: grave-digging (lay men), laying the body out (women), baking refreshments and minding the children (of course, the women). It is only when we get to the cooking and the childcare that gender is explicitly mentioned – 'women's work'. However, gender is implied in the previous tasks, with interestingly contrasting explanations. The minister will not dig the hole because 'others who are stronger and weaker will have to do that'. Men are assumed to be stronger (than women? or than the minister?), but perhaps that only relates to physical labour – in other ways they are weaker, because there are some important things they can't do. The minister will not clean the corpse's face, because 'others who are weaker and stronger will have to do that'. Women are assumed to be the weaker sex, and yet they are also stronger, because handling death so intimately requires courage and resilience. It is as if each gender, and then the minister, who almost stands in a different place altogether, has their inexorable tasks that they 'have to do' at this time.

A second two-line announcement reveals what the minister's role is: it is 'to come/ and take care of the words'. Like the three repetitions of 'he won't' above, there are three statements beginning 'he doesn't have to'. Once again, the significance of what he does do with the words is led up to by repeated negatives. Again, there is a sense that necessity controls what goes on here; it is not about the decisions or preferences of individual people. This does rather challenge our current interests in liturgy, especially at funerals, where there is usually an effort to be creative and individual, depending on the beliefs and character of the one who has died. But here it is strongly affirmed that the minister's feelings, preferences or even performance standards are strictly irrelevant. He doesn't have to make words up, say them well or even like them – 'so long as they agree to *obey* him'. This arresting assertion actually puts its finger on exactly what makes a liturgy in the presence of death work. The minister has to 'hold' the event with a genuine authority if the congregation is to feel safe. Anyone who has experienced a funeral that was incompetently led in this sense will be aware what an unsettling and unsatisfactory experience it was.

But the image that the poem uses to express this disturbing possibility focuses not on the congregation but on the words themselves. It is as if they are a flock of ghostly spirits who do not know 'where to go', but circle around and around 'the confusing cemetery' (populated by a very large number of the dead) instead of settling with the grave of this person. We are left with an image of restless spirits who roam the earth like flocks of birds, unable to be 'earthed' by an appropriate laying to rest. The image calls on many resonances, including some biblical ones. In the Gospels, Jesus is shown as having authority over rebellious or unhappy spirits, and sometimes he instructs them where to go to defuse their destructive power (for example in Mark 5). But many other societies have imagined that the period during which a dead body is ritually disposed of is a time of liminality and danger, and that there is a possibility that discarnate spirits will be released. This is the origin of the belief in and fear of ghosts, and we seem to be in the same realm as in the last stanza of 'Fidele's Dirge' (p. 15).

Winter Camping

One thing was always understood between us.
When you were ready to go Winter Camping
I would not be a part of the adventure.

You bought equipment and wrote plans in journals,
Calling it Personal Development,
Anticipating solitude and challenge.

You never did it. Life got in the way
Until death stopped the prospect altogether.
I have not often thought about it since.

Sleeping without you was a big adventure.
A single bed, electrically warmed,
Beside the open door onto the balcony.

Birds visited. Various gastropods
Slid over the threshold and were welcome.
Cats came and went. Last night there was a storm.

I went to sleep enchanted by the wind.
It died in the small hours; the silence woke me.
I am in an extraordinary place.

Dark, starred with tiny lights across the valley,
Clouded with frozen breath. I move carefully,
Explore the limits of my warm cocoon.

Now on my left there is a precipice.
Cold fingers trace the edges of my ears.
I am alone and this is Winter Camping.

Ann Drysdale

Ann Drysdale lives and writes in Wales, but grew up in England
and spent some of her life as a hill farmer on the moors of North
Yorkshire. She has written a number of poems about her partner's
terminal cancer, and the poem 'Winter Camping' explores a particu-
lar stage of fairly early grief. Feeling cold is a common experience
for the bereaved, but Drysdale explores this theme in an unusual and
personal way, woven in with particular memories about the dead
man, and what his plans and dreams had been.

113

The poem is conversational in tone, and structured with little three-line stanzas that do not rhyme, and it starts straight in with a no-nonsense memory of an implicit 'deal' that the partners had: 'One thing was always understood between us' – namely, that any plans about going 'Winter Camping' (note the emphatic, possibly ironic capital letters) were *not* going to include the speaker. It was his dream adventure, and absolutely not hers. There is a sense that the notion of 'Winter Camping' was part of the ongoing implicit dialogue between a couple who were close, but aware of entertaining different ambitions and fantasies. So what the title stands for is a very particular memory of their intimate relationship, even if it calls forth a certain rolling of the eyes. You already have the feeling that the speaker had a certain scepticism all along as to whether this adventure would ever actually take place, even if equipment was purchased, plans devised and the mind and heart apparently prepared for the challenge.

Who knows whether the plan was something that really would have happened, if cancer had not intervened – or always a pipe-dream that represented a vague desire for adventure that was unlikely to be tested in reality. 'Life got in the way' until death definitely brought the project to an end. Apparently the notion was not that important, since 'I have not often thought about it since'. Nevertheless, the reader has been alerted that there is something telling in this memory, which will be explored further. The nonchalant tone belies what the poem may turn out to be about.

The fourth stanza introduces a different kind of challenge, which has been necessarily undertaken by the speaker (it is implied since the death). But there is actually a sense of excitement about what this has been like: 'Sleeping without you was a big adventure'. Of course, most people who have been bereaved of their partners feel it acutely when there is suddenly no one else in the big bed with them, and many would express how painful or lonely this is. Not so this speaker. It appears that she has altered her sleeping arrangements dramatically. She has started to sleep in a single bed, and (strangely) decided to leave the balcony door open so that the outside world, including cold and stormy weather, can permeate her sleeping space. The bed is heated by an electric blanket to enable her to stay warm enough to let this happen.

The next two stanzas recount, in very short sentences, the events of her extraordinary nights. Other creatures make their entrance, some of which might be expected, like cats, others perhaps more surprising, such as birds. You have the feeling that a kind of comfort and kinship is experienced in relation to other living things, who 'visit' as if they had the power to assuage human loneliness. Even the snails and slugs are afforded hospitality. We are shown the 'Various gastropods' sliding over the line ending just as they slid into the bedroom from the balcony, 'and were welcome'. The storm was an event to be marvelled at rather than suffered. 'I went to sleep enchanted by the wind'; there is something magical about this curious time of going through bereavement. When the wind died ('in the small hours' – perhaps her partner had too) 'the silence woke me' – rather as the silence that death brings has the power to do. Yet there is a sense of gift and wonder in the experience; waking in the small hours leaves the speaker 'in an extraordinary place'. From her perspective in bed, looking out of the balcony door, she can see the starry night sky, the valley, and her own frozen breath between her and the view. She has to be careful about moving and letting her bed cool down; but you have the sense that exploring 'the limits of my warm cocoon' is about more than sleeping arrangements – it is about moving gingerly, as a mourner does, within the places of psychic safety that she constructs in which memories can be held and grief may be worked through.

The potential danger of exposing her psyche too much is implied in the final stanza: 'Now on my left there is a precipice'. On the side where the body of her loved companion used to be there is not just a cold space, but somewhere she feels she could fall right down and be destroyed. No warm fingers of a lover but 'cold fingers' of the icy temperature in the room 'trace the edges of my ears'. This observation is acute, combining accuracy about which extremities get the coldest most quickly, and tenderness about the remembered touch of the beloved. The final line brings us round to the starting point: 'I am alone and this is Winter Camping'. It is not the partner but the poem's narrator (who never wanted this kind of adventure in the first place) who is actually undertaking Winter Camping. And the excitement and dreams of her beloved have transferred themselves to her, helping her get through the early part of her bereavement (which, of course, she would never have chosen to experience) in a way that includes enchantment along with the pain.

(VII) Familiar

Call it unfortunate if you will – I
Can certainly understand why –
But love is so persistent. It just goes on
After, you might reasonably say, its usefulness is done,
However silent the house, empty the bed,
Obsequies long since over, long since buried the dead.

Love is a damaged thing, trailing absurd,
Forlorn and pathetic as a dressing-gown cord.
Intimate as breath, loyal as a shadow, close as a cry,
Nothing will shake it off.

Nor should you try.

R. V. Bailey

R. V. Bailey's long-term partner was the poet U. A. Fanthorpe (see p. 104), and this brief poem is part of a sequence tracing the progress of Fanthorpe's last illness and death. It pinpoints, in an understated but telling way, an aspect of grief that is very recognizable to those who have lost someone deeply loved. The poem by Carol Ann Duffy (p. 97) explores the great difficulty that is often experienced initially by the bereaved in coming to terms with the fact of death. This poem is set rather later in the process of bereavement, after facts have been fully accepted – and yet the heart continues to persist in love towards someone who is no longer there to receive it. This sense of love having nowhere to go seems to come about even if the mourner has a belief in life after death, since the love arises from the earthly experience of the beloved and cannot really be separated from its earthbound origin.

The poem is divided into two parts, and consists of rhymed couplets that are not even in their rhythm. The rhymes have the effect of a sort of gentle, self-teasing humour, until the end, when they emphasize a certain assurance and pride.

The tone of the first half of the poem is conversational and self-deprecatory; rather than describing the romantic depths of passion, it forms a wry observation on something that cannot be changed and might even be regarded as 'unfortunate'. The speaker (the hapless sufferer of continuing love) even claims to be able to understand why people might think that. The reader is alerted, though, by the poem's apparent nonchalance, that something extremely important is going to be announced, and so it is: 'love is so persistent'. This statement is a far cry from traditional, inspiring assertions about love's enduring power, such as 'love is strong as death' (Song of Songs 8.6). For it reveals that when you actually experience this, it is a very mixed blessing. It is hard to see what good it is to the person who has died, and for the person who survives it can be a painful nuisance. Others reach a point where they cannot understand why the bereaved person still seems so deeply bound up with the person who has died, and the mourner can in principle sympathize with this position. Love 'just goes on/ After, you might reasonably say, its usefulness is done'. There is, it seems, no *point* to this love that endures even though the house is silent, the bed empty, the funeral finished and the body buried.

The second half of this brief poem shifts tone. It is no longer reasonable and distanced, no longer trying to adopt the view of the ordinary person outside the situation who might reckon that it is time to move on and have some closure. (It is fatally easy to come to that conclusion on behalf of someone else.) The first two lines of this section are effectively a shameless cry of agony: 'Love is a damaged thing, trailing absurd,/ Forlorn and pathetic as a dressing-gown cord'. This brilliant image, of the drooping and quite possibly fraying dressing-gown cord trailing uselessly along, pinpoints precisely how absurd the love appears now to be. And there is an implication that the grieving owner of the dressing gown may have been spending an inordinate amount of time herself not bothering to get dressed properly because there is no longer any point.

But then the tone shifts again, perhaps prompted by other intimate and routine memories associated with being around the home together in relaxed and comfy clothes. It is as if the persistent love has taken on the wonderful and protective qualities that a loved dressing gown can also have. Love is 'Intimate as breath, loyal as a shadow, close as a cry'. The bereaved may not always need to go around in sleepwear, but she has to breathe, she has to carry around her shadow, and it is sometimes necessary to cry. And so we reach the conclusion, which is two half-lines, deliberately divided by a line space to give the reader time for a breath: 'Nothing will shake it off/ Nor should you try'. That you cannot rid yourself of love (which could be a cry of exasperation) is in fact a matter of pride, comfort and self-identity. It is just so 'familiar'; it is like a 'familiar'; it is your second self, and it goes on being vital to you beyond the apparent full stop of the death of the one you love.

REMEMBERING
AND CELEBRATING

Parted

Farewell to one now silenced quite,
Sent out of hearing, out of sight, –
　My friend of friends, whom I shall miss.
　He is not banished, though, for this, –
Nor he, nor sadness, nor delight.

Though I shall talk with him no more,
A low voice sounds upon the shore.
　He must not watch my resting-place,
　But who shall drive a mournful face
From the sad winds about my door?

I shall not hear his voice complain,
But who shall stop the patient rain?
　His tears must not disturb my heart,
　But who shall change the years, and part
The world from every thought of pain?

Although my life is left so dim,
The morning crowns the mountain-rim;
　Joy is not gone from summer skies,
　Nor innocence from children's eyes,
And all these things are part of him.

He is not banished, for the showers
Yet wake this green warm earth of ours.
　How can the summer but be sweet?
　I shall not have him at my feet,
And yet my feet are on the flowers.

Alice Meynell

The poems in the last section address the sharp details of quite early bereavement, but those in this part of the book have been chosen to convey the rather more distanced, celebratory perspective that can emerge later on. Grief changes with time, as those who mourn begin to incorporate the beloved dead into their own continuing lives, allowing the dead to influence and inhabit their own gaze upon the world.

This poem by Alice Meynell apparently belongs in this category. Certainly I chose it because it seems to be about coming to terms with life after suffering the death of a beloved man, and I still believe that this is the most natural reading of the poem. However, looking at her biography, there is another possibility. Meynell was received into the Roman Catholic Church at about the age of 21, and experienced a hopeless but intense passion for the priest who instructed her in the faith. Both of them realized that they needed to create distance between them, and some of Meynell's poetry at that time (for instance 'After a Parting' and 'Renunciation') are certainly about the effort to relinquish this inappropriate relationship. It is possible that 'Parted' is in the same sequence of poems; but it is very convincing as a portrait of being parted by death.

The poem is written in five-line stanzas, with a regular rhyme scheme (AABBA). The rhythm is steady, with four pulses in each line, rather like a heartbeat. Pain is referred to; there are tears and mournfulness. But the overall tone is of bearing the loss now not just with endurance but with a growing recognition that life still includes the capacity for joy, and that the beloved, though irremediably absent, is also somehow present in a new way.

The first stanza speaks farewell to 'one now silenced quite'. Surely this is about the dead – though other terms do suggest a kind of banishment: 'Sent out of hearing, out of sight'. The highlighting of bodily senses suggests a kind of love that was tender and physical, even though the description of the relationship could be platonic: 'My friend of friends, whom I shall miss'. But perhaps this is a careful, passionate reserve. It seems to be stated that the banishment (real or metaphorical) is not because of the friendship. The strange last line yokes together the man himself with contrasting, even ambivalent responses in her. Neither sadness nor delight are banished; they are woven together, as the rest of the poem shows.

The second and third stanzas suggest both his absence in body and his continuing reality in the speaker's landscape. There will be no more conversation, but 'A low voice sounds upon the shore' – presumably the endless, repeated sound of waves breaking. The man himself will not meet her where she lives, but it is as if the wind around her door itself has 'mournful face' that can never be dismissed. His actual voice will not be heard again, 'But who shall stop the patient rain?' This thought is extended as the wetness of gentle rain (there is nothing wild or stormy about it) merges into 'His tears'. The final question in this verse is a rhetorical one. Time will change the disturbance in her heart, but will not eradicate all thoughts of grief, which seems to have taken up residence in the created world itself.

The fourth verse appears to start in a gloomy and diminished way ('my life is left so dim'), but is actually the turning point where joy starts to break in. The dimness is like the moments before dawn, when 'The morning crowns the mountain-rim'. And classically inspiring parts of life, like summer skies and the faces of children, now mysteriously return to the speaker's consciousness as being 'part of him'.

The final stanza is immensely strong. 'He is not banished' is a powerful assertion, whether it is about an enforced separation in life or is stated in the face of death. There is an intense sweetness and physicality about the speaker's appreciation of the growing spring daylight, with both warmth and rain: 'the showers/ Yet wake this green warm earth of ours'. The earth is not just hers but 'ours'; she feels connected and alive like the rest of creation. She cannot and does not wish to deny the beauty and delight of summer, even without the presence of her beloved. (Immediate grief can certainly make everything appear grey and pointless, or inappropriately and heartlessly brash.)

And the final two lines embody a kind of genuine acceptance of both loss and continuing life. The repetition of 'my feet' brings home the balance that has been achieved. Neither grief nor delight in beauty is to be denied: 'I shall not have him at my feet,/ And yet my feet are on the flowers.'

Clearances III

When all the others were away at Mass
I was all hers as we peeled potatoes.
They broke the silence, let fall one by one
Like solder weeping off the soldering iron:
Cold comforts set between us, things to share
Gleaming in a bucket of clean water.
And again let fall. Little pleasant splashes
From each other's work would bring us to our senses.

So while the parish priest at her bedside
Went hammer and tongs at the prayers for the dying
And some were responding and some crying
I remembered her head bent towards my head,
Her breath in mine, our fluent dipping knives –
Never closer the whole rest of our lives.

Seamus Heaney

In this beautiful little sonnet, the poet recalls both his mother's deathbed and a vivid memory of an intimate moment with her where they felt very connected. Heaney, who became a Nobel laureate for his poetry, wrote many poems in which he explored what it meant to be highly educated and articulate within a family of origin where others were not. Sometimes he describes scenes where in order to fit in he feels he has to hold back on what he knows or how he would normally converse. So it is interesting that the memory he describes is a scene where he is helping his mother to perform a chore she is expert in, and in which it is completely unnecessary to speak.

The first eight lines of the sonnet (the octet) set the scene in a typical Irish home, where the majority of the household are out at Mass, and the poet and his mother are on their own at home preparing the Sunday dinner. The introductory line, 'When all the others were away at Mass', leaves a great deal unsaid. Perhaps this is a regular habit, and both mother and son had already been to Mass, early in the morning. Perhaps it's an unusual event, and this is a small boy who is not very well and his mum has stayed home from church to look after him. Or maybe this is a memory of a grown man who is home for a visit, and has long since given up attending Mass himself.

Certainly the less than enthusiastic description of the priest in the second part of the poem would be consistent with that.

'I was all hers as we peeled potatoes'. In a large Catholic family (Seamus was one of nine children), managing to carve out some personal one-to-one space with your mother would have been unusual and memorable. You wonder, if this is a childhood memory, whether the speaker really means 'she was all mine' for once. But if this is an adult memory, he could well be seeking to achieve a momentary connection where he is concentrating wholly on 'being there' for his mother, who found him rather intimidating and difficult to understand. The silence, the not needing to speak, is only broken by the splashes into the water of the potatoes they each let fall. The image of the solder coming off the soldering iron is interesting and arresting. Visually, it takes us into a quite different kind of focused activity – more traditionally masculine. It reminds us that preparing vegetables is (to his mother) not really a man's job, so for him to help with it suggests a deliberate kind of seeking to get close. Soldering irons, of course, are used to create lasting connections. But the excess pieces of solder don't just drop, they weep. There is pain here that suggests the adult man's awareness of his complicated relationship with his mother.

The description of the naked potatoes themselves as 'cold comforts' continues this thought. Peeled potatoes are indeed cold, and yet their growing number in the bucket of cold water represents a shared achievement, and they gleam with it. They are 'set between us', a phrase that simultaneously conveys a shared practical task and a sense of something that divides the two people. But then we are brought back to the simple, physical enjoyment of a task that literally connects them through mutual splashes of water: 'Little pleasant splashes/ From each other's work would bring us to our senses'. That proverbial phrase is made fresh by the sensory nature of the experience, but it also implies that there is here a refuge from the ambivalent dynamic that divergence in language and lifestyle over time have brought.

The sestet moves to the mother's deathbed, at which the speaker is presumably present, though in a distanced way, observing dispassionately what is going on in the bedroom. Again the poet deploys a familiar cliché to powerful effect. The depiction of the prayers for the dying being conducted in a 'hammer and tongs' way is unexpected.

There is perhaps an implication that what should be gentle, quiet and moving is actually being delivered at breakneck speed, and with small regard for the actual individual who is dying. In any case, a routine 'hammer and tongs' delivery of the sacrament implies a huge contrast with the weeping soldering iron, or with the 'fluent dipping knives' the speaker recalls from the potato-peeling episode. The poem has occasional rhymes and half-rhymes, and here the 'prayers for the dying' are matched by 'some crying' – as if those who can't any longer believe or recite the prayer responses resort to tears as their only way of participating. Certainly the speaker finds vivid refuge in mentally escaping the conventional religious scenario by recalling the almost sacramental intimacy that had been achieved in the context of a very ordinary everyday activity between mother and son.

For the final images of the poem evoke the memory that is precious and lasting. In such a way, as grief moves on, survivors make choices about the kinds of memory they want to dwell on, and those they leave behind. We are not shown anything about how the woman herself approached her death. Rather, we are left once more with the pleasures of that shared activity in the kitchen. The physical closeness of the participants conveys their emotional connection at that time, which itself echoes earlier experiences of being mothered in infancy, with heads bent towards one another and breathing intertwined. The final end-rhymed couplet exudes satisfaction in a relationship affirmed: 'I remembered her head bent towards my head,/ Her breath in mine, our fluent dipping knives –/ Never closer the whole rest of our lives.'

Jewels in my Hand

I hold dead friends like jewels in my hand
Watching their brilliance gleam against my palm
Turquoise and emerald, jade, a golden band.

All ravages of time they can withstand
Like talismans their grace keeps me from harm
I hold dead friends like jewels in my hand.

I see them standing in some borderland
Their heads half-turned, waiting to take my arm
Turquoise and emerald, jade, a golden band.

I'm not afraid they will misunderstand
My turning to them like a magic charm
I hold dead friends like jewels in my hand
Turquoise and emerald, jade, a golden band.

Sasha Moorsom

Sasha Moorsom was accomplished in many areas of life. She was one of the first women producers in the BBC, and brought the poems of people like Ted Hughes and Philip Larkin to a Radio 3 audience long before they were well known. This poem, like Dylan Thomas' 'Do not go gentle into that good night' (p. 78), is in the form of a villanelle, with only two end-rhymes throughout, and two repeated 'refrain' lines, which alternate from verse to verse. But its tone and character could not be more different from Thomas' poem. In her later years, Moorsom was apparently influenced and comforted by the philosophy of Buddhism, and there is a peacefulness about this poem that suggests a willingness to let things be as they are, rather than a desire to strive and struggle against the ravages of death.

The speaker, like the dead friends she remembers, is evidently a woman who has reached an age when it is quite normal to have a whole company of friends among your beloved dead. It is usually the generation above you who dies first, and while there is a very specific grief for parents and grandparents, especially if the deaths were sudden or premature, or if you still depended on them in crucial ways, the sequence feels 'normal'. It is initially rare for members of your peer group or younger to die, and at first these are still exceptional, but after a time there may be more of your dear friends who have died than remain alive. The implications for yourself and your own mortality are steadily harder to ignore, and it becomes quite simply lonely, as chosen intimates who represented part of your identity and a significant part of your past fall away. Less has been said, perhaps, about the impact of the death of friends than about being bereaved of your parent, partner or child.

'I hold dead friends like jewels in my hand'. There is a calm slowness about the poem, which echoes the sense of permanence suggested by the 'jewels'. This is not about one particular bereavement, but calls forth a group of people whose deaths have been sufficiently incorporated by the speaker for her memories to have crystallized. The fact that a whole number of friends can be recalled, held and gazed at together should have the effect of making them seem smaller or of less individual significance, but I think the opposite is true. What comes over is a powerful sense of the beauty and preciousness of the friends, both as distinct individuals and as a connected group – perhaps we are even to imagine that the speaker is handling a bracelet that literally holds together a variety of different and valuable stones. Or it may be that each friend is like a distinct jewel, held in the palm of the hand with several others. The uniqueness of each friend is symbolized by the quite different kinds of precious stone (though, interestingly, turquoise, emerald and jade are all usually shades of green). I am not sure whether 'a golden band' is a wedding ring that is also included, or is a reference to a golden group of these assorted friends. 'Watching their brilliance gleam against my palm' conveys a sense of the rich jewels (which are securely undying, in contrast with the mortal flesh of the palm that holds them). But to me it speaks of feisty and brilliant women, who perhaps as a group in the course of life evoked and reflected back each other's lively conversation and responses of friendship. Although she has lost them, there is a way in which the speaker is able to capture and hold the memories of those interactions with her, and so have them in a form that can never be lost.

The second stanza takes up the idea of permanence (possible only now that they are dead): 'All ravages of time they can withstand'. This is, of course, not yet possible for the speaker, who remains alive and with all the vulnerability of the mortal. And yet she states that 'Like talismans their grace keeps me from harm', before returning to repeat the opening line about holding them in her hand. Many people facing illness find that a certain object, kept with them through dangerous times, can provide a sense of comfort; it might be a holding cross or a smooth stone, or a photo or soft toy. Usually the object will have particular and reassuring significance. Whether personal or religious, such objects are often reminders about being loved. Perhaps the speaker has in fact been given gifts of jewellery by her friends. This speaker imagines her dead friends as if they were, together, a set of talismanic objects like this, which can never be lost to her or taken away. The poem is beginning to have the feel of a spell of protection, in which the repetitions and the chanted rhymes mirror this comforting arena of safety.

The third stanza says a little more about the women, who move from being conceived as jewels to being shadowy figures who have gone ahead of the speaker, and are waiting 'in some borderland', half looking back at her and 'waiting to take my arm'. It is as if they are gathering together to go out as a group, and are expecting the speaker to come and link arms with them to go on. Here the poem explicitly acknowledges the reality that the speaker will, of course, eventually (perhaps soon) join them in the realm of death. But the context suggests that this is normal, comfortable and companionable – not something to be fearful about. To pass over into the realm of death will be to link quite naturally with one's old friends again – and move on.

The final verse steps back slightly, recognizing that this 'spell' may sound slightly odd in a contemporary context. But perhaps, just as they were accommodating of each other's quirks and fears in life, these beloved women will not 'misunderstand/ My turning to them like a magic charm'. We have a sense of the bonds of amused affection continuing beyond death. The kind of comfort and safety such remembered 'jewels' can offer is clearly not about preventing the speaker from having one day to face death herself. But it is about taking away all anxiety about that.

Into the Hour

I have come into the hour of a white healing.
Grief's surgery is over and I wear
The scar of my remorse and of my feeling.

I have come into a sudden sunlit hour
When ghosts are scared to corners. I have come
Into the time when grief begins to flower

Into a new love. It had filled my room
Long before I recognized it. Now
I speak its name. Grief finds its good way home.

The apple-blossom's handsome on the bough
And Paradise spreads round. I touch its grass.
I want to celebrate but don't know how.

I need not speak though everyone I pass
Stares at me kindly. I would put my hand
Into their hands. Now I have lost my loss

In some way I may later understand.
I hear the singing of the summer grass.
And love, I find, has no considered end,

Nor is it subject to the wilderness
Which follows death. I am not traitor to
A person or a memory. I trace

Behind that love another which is running
Around, ahead. I need not ask its meaning.

Elizabeth Jennings

Elizabeth Jennings was born in Boston, Lincolnshire, though as an adult she spent most of her time in Oxford. She was raised a Catholic, and moral and spiritual issues and a habit of acute, sensitive self-examination remained vital elements of her poetry. She said of religion that it was 'a real and important part of my life, and because it was important, it tended to give me a lot of worries'. She never married, though there was an early engagement and relationships with various men, including one that was very significant but had to be given up. She experienced periods of profound mental distress and spent time in psychiatric care and treatment.

This poem explores that stage of grief when, after a long period in which it seems that the burden of sorrow will never lift, the bereaved person finds that something has moved on and that life contains a new flowering of energy and even joy. The tone of the poem is reflective and slightly surprised, with a conversational rhythm that feels quite unstructured, as if the speaker is making a series of remarks just as they occur to her, as she gently probes and tries to articulate what is the state of her psyche now. But on inspection we see that it is a very carefully constructed text, with a series of three-line verses where the first and third lines rhyme (or almost rhyme), and the middle line introduces a word at the end that is then picked up and echoed in the next stanza. So the stanzas are sort of stitched together, rather as the speaker is stitching together her previously fractured soul. Eventually there is a half-rhyming couplet at the end, which sums up the progress that has been reached and points ahead to the future.

The poem begins with imagery of a hospital. The phrase 'white healing' is curious, suggesting perhaps a hospital room that is either sunlit or surrounded with blank walls. Or she may be referring to her body, which is white from staying indoors during a convalescence. It is not clear yet whether the state she is about to describe is a positive one, or just rather bloodless. 'Grief's surgery' pinpoints where she has been. It is a brilliant metaphor, suggesting both the sharpness of grief and its necessity – and, indeed, how major it is, how deeply it penetrates the body as well as the heart. The consequent scars (which she describes herself as wearing) convey both successful healing and the permanent marks of what has happened. It is interesting that 'remorse' is part of grief's heritage, whatever or whoever has been mourned.

In the next stanza she twice repeats the poem's opening phrase 'I have come', which asserts her own progress and agency in this process (but also a sense of wonder that it can be true). Now there is definitely sunlight, suddenly occurring, sweeping fears to go to huddle in corners rather than dominate the heart. A new metaphor for grief, utterly different from that of surgery, emerges. Now it is a growing plant, which 'begins to flower/ Into a new love'. The sentence carries right over from one verse to the next, to mirror the unstoppable power of organic growth. It is as if this growth has happened unnoticed, and it is only now it is already filling the room that 'I speak its name'. And then there is a sentence of enormous comfort to all who go through the process of mourning. No longer a flower, it has become a person; or rather, perhaps, it has become one with the person who suffers it, and 'Grief finds its good way home'.

This assertion gives way to the paean of praise in the next verse, which rejoices in apple-blossom 'handsome on the bough' (an interestingly masculine adjective, resisting any sense of cute prettiness), and there are echoes of Eden: 'Paradise spreads round'. The speaker seems to feel that she has been restored to a kind of innocence or primeval beauty as she touches the grass on the early summer day, which has either only just warmed the earth and brought out the blossom or has been there unnoticed by her. In her vulnerable state, so lately trapped in grief and distress, 'I want to celebrate but don't know how'. This awkwardness continues, as she finds herself inarticulate and imagines being stared at (albeit kindly) by whoever passes. She wishes to connect with them but cannot work out what is appropriate, on a day when she feels new-minted, but they may feel that everything is ordinary.

The phrase 'Now I have lost my loss/ In some way I may later understand' is arresting, and absolutely authentic to the experience of grief, as time passes. The mourner longs to be delivered from the waves of pain, the unending absorption, the sheer boredom of grief – and yet there is something comforting about holding on to the loss and its significance to your soul. Something feels wrong when the loss is forgotten, or becomes less sharp and real. And yet it is as important to let yourself experience this shift (understood or not) as it was to address the grief head on initially. New things, or old things newly perceived, can be let in again: 'I hear the singing of the summer grass'. Like R. V. Bailey's poem (p. 116), this seeks to express how love does not really end, as it rationally should, with death. Neither does it simply peter out into 'the wilderness/ Which follows death'. During the desert of early grief there is indeed a feeling that to let yourself love again, or even to feel wholehearted joy again, would be a kind of treachery towards the loved one who has died. But gradually it becomes clear that this is not so.

The final couplet, about another love 'which is running/ Around, ahead' could be describing the blossoming of a new relationship, which the speaker of the poem is finally ready to be open to. Or it could be the mysterious, divine love at the heart of creation, which is once again experienced as joyous and good. As the poem remarks, 'I need not ask its meaning'.

The Change

For years the dead
were the terrible weight of their absence,
the weight of what one had not put in their hands.
Rarely a visitation – dream or vision –
lifted that load for a moment, like someone
standing behind one and briefly taking
the heft of a frameless pack.
But the straps remained, and the ache –
though you can learn not to feel it
except when malicious memory
pulls downward with sudden force.
Slowly there comes a sense
that for some time the burden
has been what you need anyway.
How flimsy to be without it, ungrounded, blown
hither and thither, colliding with stern solids.
And then they begin to return, the dead:
but not as visions. They're not
separate now, not to be seen, no,
it's they who see: they displace,
for seconds, for minutes, maybe longer,
the mourner's gaze with their own. Just now,
that shift of light, arpeggio
on ocean's harp –
not the accustomed bearer
of heavy absence saw it, it was perceived
by the long-dead, long absent, looking
out from within one's wideopen eyes.

Denise Levertov

This poem also explores that stage of grief where things are changing within the psyche of the bereaved in a profound way. Something different is happening over time to the loss that has been suffered. Like Sasha Moorsom's poem (p. 127), it speaks about 'the dead' as a company, rather than about a particular loss. It has become possible to generalize and to understand something about how one is affected by all of one's beloved dead. We never discover in this poem even what the relationships in life had been, whether they were of the older generation or a mixture of ages. What they have in common is that death was not recent; its reality has been true 'For years'.

The controlling image of the first part of the poem is that of weight – 'the terrible weight of their absence' – and the sense of remorse or guilt about what the bereaved knows she did not give to the relationship in life: 'the weight of what one had not put in their hands'. It is an arresting thought that it is precisely two kinds of nothingness – things that are not there, and things that did not happen – that seem to create the burden that weighs so heavily on the speaker. She then introduces the idea of a 'visitation' (the word has a semi-religious air of significance and mystery), but it is something that is not quite seen by the person visited. It is as if someone behind them 'lifted that load for a moment' by taking the 'heft' of the pack carried on their back. It is not exactly that the burden was lifted right off, for the feeling of the straps, and the 'ache' of the weight were still there. The speaker then muses how you can learn to ignore that feeling 'except when malicious memory/ pulls downward with sudden force'. This detailed and accurate description of how grief can be semi-forgotten and then suddenly renewed very sharply by a trick of memory is brilliant in this context, continuing as it does the image of the heavy backpack. To tug downwards on someone's backpack is indeed a cruel prank and would take them painfully unawares.

In the centre of the poem the speaker begins to describe how things start to change in relation to the burden – not that it goes away exactly, but that you sense 'that for some time the burden/ has been what you need anyway'. You realize that you would feel 'flimsy' without it, 'ungrounded'. I think this is partly about the necessity of grief as the cost of love, rather than an unhealthy desire to cling to a kind of pain or loss that needs to be let go of. Or perhaps it is about the sense that responding powerfully to a death has put you in touch with what is the grounded nature of mortal life; no longer is it possible to live as if we did not die, or were able to dwell in a purely abstract realm. Or perhaps it is about being aware of needing to incorporate within one's own psyche the lives of the beloved dead.

Certainly the next line picks up this idea, as the dead 'begin to return . . . but not as visions'. There is a gradual reversal of perspective. Of course, the poem is charting changes that are happening within the mourner, but they are described as if it is the dead who are the agents of these changes. Instead of being perceived as separate beings who could in some way return in memory or vision, they are no longer to be seen: 'no,/ it's they who see'. There is a sense that they have displaced the seeing gaze of the mourner with their own. They have taken over the mourner's capacity to look outwards, and for the first time in the poem the focus is not on the burdensome experience of the one suffering grief, but the sudden luminous beauty of the world, 'that shift of light, arpeggio/ on ocean's harp'. It is only a momentary shaft of observation, but the mixture of light, ocean and a shiver of harp music suggests something joyful and transcendent, a blend of earth and heaven.

And so the experience of noticing sheer, piercing beauty again (as in the previous poem) marks a moment when there is a profound shift for the mourner. Previously, 'the accustomed bearer/ of heavy absence' was presumably unable to lift her gaze to take in aspects of the world that could give joy. But now, it is as if the dead are within her and looking out from her own 'wideopen eyes'. Potentially a rather alarming idea, the description of this gradual shift in perspective comes over as a comforting observation of the way in which grief does, over time, allow for the dead to live again within the heart of the mourner, and deeply influence what the world looks like now.

The Plumber

Harry Patch (1898–2009)

He'd often work crouched on the floor
his toolbag agape beside him
like a wound.

He'd choose spanner or wrench,
tap for an airlock, blockage, leak,
for water's sound.

Not a man for talk. His work
a translation, his a clean trade
for silent hands.

Sweet water washed away waste,
the mud, the blood, the dirt,
the dead, the drowned,

the outcry, outfall, outrage of war
transformed
to holy ground.

Gillian Clarke

The last two poems in this section honour individuals who have died but were not known personally to the authors. Rather, their presence in the public domain has given their deaths a wider, iconic significance, and this is what is celebrated.

Harry Patch lived to be 111 years old, and he was the very last surviving British veteran of the First World War. Remarkably, he declined to speak about his wartime experiences until he was over 100, when he was approached for a television programme. Born in 1898, he was wounded at the battle of Passchendaele in September 1917, when he lost three friends. In 2007 he published his memoirs, *The Last Fighting Tommy*, and recalled that when faced with a German soldier, and recalling the Ten Commandments ('Thou shalt not kill'), he took care to wound but not kill him. He described war as the 'calculated and condoned slaughter of human beings', and said that 'it isn't worth one life'. When he was 107, he met and shook hands with a similarly aged German veteran. At his funeral he specified that there should be no guns.

Patch's profession was that of a plumber. Among other projects, he worked on the construction of the Wills building in Bristol. This is now part of the University of Bristol, who later gave Patch an honorary degree in the same building he had helped to plumb. Gillian Clarke focuses on the image of how an ordinary plumber does his work, implying that the work of construction that happened after the wars of the twentieth century is the true and honourable heritage of a remarkable man.

The poem is made up of five short, succinct stanzas, where you feel that there is not a single unnecessary extra word; this seems fitting to describe a man who was not one for talk. Each stanza ends with a short, blunt line that speaks directly to the point. There is nothing abstract or vague about what is depicted; it is detailed, practical and intimate. The horrors of the war he fought in are present, but in a very restrained way. It starts straight in with a picture of Patch at work; like many plumbers, he is 'crouched' in order to access the pipes that provide for the cleanliness of modern living. His old-fashioned toolbag would have been made of leather, its zip open ('agape beside him') to give access to different tools as required for the job. As the speaker remarks, it is 'like a wound'. This reminds us of the terrible wounds he had to crouch beside in battle, as he saw his friends' bodies taken apart in the mud.

The second stanza shows him attending closely to the task in hand, selecting the right tool, tapping the pipes, listening carefully for where the problem lay. Often it is a long job detecting exactly where water is blocked or leaking in a pipe system. Practical as this point is, the reader is made aware that 'water's sound' may have a symbolic significance, and this begins to be revealed in the next stanza. This reflects on his extraordinary silence for the majority of his life about what he and others suffered. Although he left it a very long time indeed before he spoke, it was common for those who returned from that war to find it impossible to communicate what they had been through to those who had not seen action. Veterans returned to their professions and rebuilt their civilian lives quietly. Working with his hands, the poem speaks of this as a 'translation' of the wartime experience, into 'a clean trade/ for silent hands'.

The 'sweet water' that is at the centre of all plumbing activity now becomes the symbol of cleansing, and a great litany of what it cleanses is begun: waste, mud, blood, dirt. In the battlefields of France and Flanders, the mud was unbelievable. Where fields were below sea level, the destruction of the drainage ditches meant that they became vast seas of mud, in which men actually drowned rather than just died from the shells. So the list continues, to include the doomed soldiers themselves, 'the dead, the drowned'. And the list continues beyond this stanza into the final one. There is a series of three words that all begin with 'out', and the metaphors of plumbing combine with the anger that this man felt about the war: 'outcry, outfall, outrage of war'.

Yet the poem claims that this work of plumbing somehow transforms the arena and outcomes of war to 'holy ground'. There are resonances of Moses' mysterious meeting with God in the desert, where he is asked to remove his shoes because he is on 'holy ground' (Exodus 3.5). So the poem starts with the plumber crouched on the floor, working, and ends, again on the ground, with a sense of hope for the future. Through its very focus on detail, the poem offers honour to someone who, because of his longevity, came to represent a whole generation of ordinary young men whose names are listed on our war memorials, but who may not otherwise be remembered.

An Arundel Tomb

Side by side, their faces blurred,
The earl and countess lie in stone,
Their proper habits vaguely shown
As jointed armour, stiffened pleat,
And that faint hint of the absurd –
The little dogs under their feet.

Such plainness of the pre-baroque
Hardly involves the eye, until
It meets his left-hand gauntlet, still
Clasped empty in the other; and
One sees, with a sharp tender shock,
His hand withdrawn, holding her hand.

They would not think to lie so long.
Such faithfulness in effigy
Was just a detail friends would see:
A sculptor's sweet commissioned grace
Thrown off in helping to prolong
The Latin names around the base.

They would not guess how early in
Their supine stationary voyage
The air would change to soundless damage,
Turn the old tenantry away;
How soon succeeding eyes begin
To look, not read. Rigidly they

Persisted, linked, through lengths and breadths
Of time. Snow fell, undated. Light
Each summer thronged the glass. A bright
Litter of birdcalls strewed the same
Bone-riddled ground. And up the paths
The endless altered people came,

Washing at their identity.
Now, helpless in the hollow of
An unarmorial age, a trough
Of smoke in slow suspended skeins

Above their scrap of history,
Only an attitude remains:

Time has transfigured them into
Untruth. The stone fidelity
They hardly meant has come to be
Their final blazon, and to prove
Our almost-instinct almost true:
What will survive of us is love.

Philip Larkin

Because of the human impulse to honour the dead, and – when we have the resources to do this – to set up monuments to remember them by, we are aware of living among generations of ancestors. Some of these we know a good deal about, because their names are among the lists of influential writers or leaders; others are only notable in our generation because there is something exceptional about their tombs. When this is the case, we may be inclined to read into the monuments and the imagined lives of the dead some of our own desires about the nature of death and the victory of love.

'An Arundel Tomb' is one of Larkin's best-known poems, the last line being independently quoted with some frequency, touching as it does precisely what our generation tends to believe can be affirmed about what happens after death. However, as we shall see, the assertion needs to be read in the light of the whole poem, where Larkin, typically, manages both to evoke tender longings while simultaneously calling into question whether we can possibly rely on them to reflect what is actually the case.

The tomb this text is responding to was created in the fourteenth century for Sir Richard FitzAlan, tenth Earl of Arundel, and his second wife Eleanor of Lancaster. It can be seen in Chichester Cathedral. It is undoubtedly the case that Larkin, who was a keen visitor of churches even though he did not approve of religion, reacted powerfully to seeing the reclining figures of the husband and wife on the tomb, unusually holding hands. He described it in a later interview as 'extremely affecting'. It is not clear quite how closely he studied the effigies or researched the history. The poem describes 'little dogs under their feet' (one is actually a lion); and he later confessed that he 'got the hands wrong – it's the right-hand gauntlet really' that Sir Richard has slipped off to hold the hand of his wife.

The story of this marriage is interesting. Richard was initially betrothed to Isabella Despenser, when they were both mere children of seven and eight, to cement the alliance of their respective fathers. In midlife, although he and Isabella had three children, Richard petitioned the Pope to annul that marriage, on the basis that they 'had been forced by blows to cohabit'. The annulment was granted (which made the children illegitimate), and Richard married Eleanor. The two undertook the traditional pilgrimage to Santiago de Compostela together. Because of this story, whatever we may think of the treatment of the first family, we know that this marriage was a love match – something not to be taken for granted in an aristocratic family of the time. In his will, Richard asked to be buried near to Eleanor, specifying that his tomb 'should be no higher than hers'.

The poem consists of seven stanzas written in a reflective and conversational tone, which is nevertheless held within a very regular pattern of six four-beat lines, and a recurring rhyme scheme (ABBCAC). Just so, the statues on the tomb combine a traditional formality of posture and clothing with a gentle intimacy that becomes the focus for the poem's reflections. These statues, gazed at today, do indeed have 'their faces blurred', because time has worn away at the stone, leaving no hint of individual expression or feature, if indeed the sculptor included any. The first stanza simply announces the rigid and undifferentiated character of these traditional memorial statues, in the 'proper habits' they would have worn in life to declare their social status. It is in the second verse that the practised eye of the visitor experiences 'a sharp tender shock' as it notices her hand, held gently in his.

Having carefully articulated our irresistible contemporary impression of what this means, the poem sets out to undermine it. The third stanza suggests that this reaction would have been far from the expectation or intention of the pair who are memorialized. 'They would not think to lie so long' must have a double meaning: that they could not have expected their tomb to survive for 600 years and still be looked upon; and that their monument is endlessly evoking in its viewers a kind of false impression. Their intimate stance would only have been seen by friends; or it was simply a 'sculptor's sweet commissioned grace'. The poem goes on seeing the passing of time through the eyes of the statues, in their 'supine stationary voyage' through the centuries, as weather, light, time and the footfall of an endlessly shifting populace take their toll. Those conjoined right hands (which formally refer to the solemn joining of hands in matrimony, but informally – especially with the gauntlet removed – seem to speak of loving, tender touch) go on declaring something to generations of 'altered people' with eyes that 'look, not read'.

It is as if our own gaze has helped to create the blurring of the faces, noted at the beginning. Our interpretation of the gesture washes at the identity of the statues, ignoring any Latin inscriptions, or any other traditional symbolism inherent in the statues and their pose, and goes straight for the poignancy of the 'attitude' that remains. The final stanza actually bluntly declares that 'Time has transfigured them into/ Untruth'. It seems like a final statement, yet even that very word 'transfigured' holds out a hope that there is more to it than a 'lie'. Something that is transfigured does indeed hold a deeper meaning than what is simply on the surface. And the speaker holds back from a definite denial of this. 'The stone fidelity/ They hardly meant' suggests it was *sort of* meant. And then the poet leads up to his final line with a characteristically hesitant qualification, 'to prove/ Our almost-instinct almost true:/ What will survive of us is love.'

Apparently Larkin scribbled at the bottom of one draft of this poem: 'Love isn't stronger than death just because statues hold hands for 600 years.' But you do feel he wished it could be.

HOPE

Death, be not Proud

Death, be not proud, though some have called thee
Mighty and dreadful, for thou art not so;
For those whom thou thinkst thou dost overthrow
Die not, poor Death, nor yet canst thou kill me.
From rest and sleep, which but thy pictures be,
Much pleasure – then, from thee much more must flow;
And soonest our best men with thee do go,
Rest of their bones and soul's delivery.
Thou'rt slave to fate, chance, kings, and desperate men,
And dost with poison, war, and sickness dwell;
And poppy or charms can make us sleep as well,
And better than thy stroke. Why swellst thou then?
One short sleep past, we wake eternally,
And death shall be no more. Death, thou shalt die.

John Donne

In the book so far, a variety of perspectives on what may lie beyond death have been presented. Many of the authors, whether fearful or resigned, have contemplated death as a final end, an entry into nothingness. Others have remained agnostic or ambiguous, or have focused on the living, and death's impact on them. In this last section, the poetry explores the theme of hope, and the majority of the writers are consciously Christian in their approach. However, this is hope that is very much in the biblical tradition of 'the conviction of things not seen' (Hebrews 11.1); clearly, we have very little evidence or information about what may lie beyond our earthly life.

Donne's sonnet 'Death, be not Proud' is perhaps one of the most famous poems about death in the English language, and it was written at a time when there was a universal belief in the existence of heaven and hell beyond earthly life. In the seventeenth century it was common to fear the judgement after death rather than (as in our own time) the process of dying itself. However, Donne's poem does not deal in the matter of judgement or personal condemnation for one's sins, but instead dwells on the ways in which death comes to us, and what our demeanour towards its ubiquity should be.

The sonnet is addressed to 'Death' itself, almost as if death were a person, an adversary to be challenged, fought and defeated. (One thinks of those traditional skeletons who dance with the living, leading people to their doom, or of the grim reaper, a shadowy figure in a cloak and hood who wields a scythe to harvest living souls.) It is important to bear in mind how much more present death was as an everyday occurrence at the time, regularly affecting every household and a wide variety of ages.

The sonnet is careful and constrained in form, with a tight rhyme scheme (ABBAABBA CDDCEE). It observes the pause between the octet and the sestet, but much the same sort of argument occurs in the second part of the poem – there is not really a profound turn after the poem's hinge. It is more of a 'and another thing' sort of development. The poem ends with an apparently triumphant couplet 'proving' the point that the speaker started with, but I am not convinced that anyone who expects one day to die is seriously comforted by this poem. It does engage with the traditional biblical promises that death has been conquered, and that it shall be no more (1 Corinthians 15.55; Revelation 21.4), but the tone of the whole thing tends to undermine any peacefulness that these promises might inspire.

First of all, the address to Death sounds like bluster: you have no reason to be proud; you think you are so 'Mighty and dreadful' – but not so; you can't kill me; 'Death, thou shalt die.' The person who is so concerned to cut 'poor Death' down to size actually sounds as if he has quite a lot to prove about the alleged powerlessness of death. Indeed, anyone who has suffered bereavement, especially repeated bereavements, cannot fail to have noticed the terrible and non-negotiable power of death to affect our lives. There is a lot to explain, and the poem takes an interesting tack. After asserting the Christian belief that we do not, in fact, die eternally (so take that, Death!), in the next four lines it argues that there must logically be actual pleasure in death. Since we derive refreshment from rest and sleep, 'which but thy pictures be', the poem's speaker argues that death (the real thing) must provide even more. Hmm. And then he points out, using a homely proverb, that the 'best men' get taken first – so presumably the company of the dead is better than that of the living. Even with that beautiful line, 'Rest of their bones and soul's delivery', which seems appropriate to the very sick or aged, it is hard to imagine that this assertion is enough to persuade us to focus our ambitions on reaching that company as soon as possible.

The sestet renews the attack on the so-called power of death, pointing out that Death has no real agency of its own, but is 'slave' to all sorts of methods and contexts that give rise to death: fate, chance, kings, desperate men, poison, war, sickness. It is a long list, but we are aware that it is not an exhaustive one. How comforting is this, in fact? There is increasingly a sense that death lurks everywhere. I find that the 'poppy or charms' (opiates and herbal remedies or spells) that 'can make us sleep as well,/ And better than thy stroke' also have a certain sinister quality. How does it come about that the speaker is dwelling now on remedies for sleeplessness: does this not bespeak the pain and fear that he is apparently keen to deny? The power and influence of death and processes that precede it, whether political, accidental, murderous or infectious, seems to be seeping into every part of this apparently confident poem, only contained by the rigorousness of the poetic form. The speaker asks, 'Why swellst thou then?' This means, why are you puffed up with pride? But the image is of one whose power does indeed keep increasing. In spite of its reassuring conclusion, and in contrast with George Herbert's poem with the same title, which follows this one, I think Donne's poem is about *timor mortis*, fear of death.

Death

Death, thou wast once an uncouth hideous thing,
    Nothing but bones,
  The sad effect of sadder groans:
Thy mouth was open, but thou couldst not sing.

For we consider'd thee as at some six
    Or ten years hence,
  After the loss of life and sense,
Flesh being turn'd to dust, and bones to sticks.

We look'd on this side of thee, shooting short;
    Where we did find
  The shells of fledge souls left behind,
Dry dust, which sheds no tears, but may extort.

But since our Saviour's death did put some blood
    Into thy face:
  Thou art grown fair and full of grace,
Much in request, much sought for, as a good.

For we do now behold thee gay and glad,
    As at doomsday;
  When souls shall wear their new array,
And all thy bones with beauty shall be clad.

Therefore we can go die as sleep, and trust
    Half that we have
  Unto an honest faithful grave;
Making our pillows either down, or dust.

George Herbert

This poem makes a fascinating comparison and contrast with the previous poem by Donne, with which it is contemporary. In this text, too, Death is addressed directly, but instead of being conceived as a feared adversary who must be defied and blustered at, to boost our courage, it is seen as a piteous, helpless thing that is eventually transformed into a joyful and resurrected body.

This poem is also very carefully structured, but in a quite different way from a sonnet. Consisting of six four-line stanzas, they follow a regular pattern of rhyme: the first and last lines rhyme with each other, as do the inner two. The metre follows a distinctive pattern. First there is a five-beat line, which begins to make an assertion; then there is a collapse into a very short two-beat line; then a four-beat line, and finally a five-beat line that matches the first line. It is as if, after the collapse, the stanza builds itself up again to pause at a significant assertion, before going on to build on this in the next stage of the poem. This makes the final line of the poem a confident climax.

Instead of the combative challenge of Donne's 'Death, be not Proud', the first line interestingly suggests that Death has somehow changed. The picture that is built up in the first two verses of the 'uncouth hideous thing' reminds us of those stone sarcophagi that display contrasting images of death. On top of the tomb lies the recumbent statue of a great person clothed in armour or bishop's robes or whatever dignities the individual achieved in life; but underneath there is a sculpture of a skeleton, lying in the same pose, which terrifyingly reminds us what is actually now in the coffin – 'Nothing but bones'. The narrator is not envisaging the dead body of a loved one who has just passed away, but that stage of death we all know that bodies reach after a number of years ('some six/ Or ten years hence'). It is 'uncouth' because it is no longer clothed in anything (including flesh) that gives dignity and individuality. It was a traditional *memento mori*, intended to urge the viewers to amend their lives while they had time. The poem presents the skeletal reality of death as hideous, sad and almost comically grotesque: 'Thy mouth wast open, but thou couldst not sing'. Of course, an empty skull often does have the jaws lying open, and there is the unsettling impression of a mirthless grin. But the inability to sing points to how the poem is about to develop. Perhaps death will come to sing and rejoice in the end.

The central two stanzas bear witness to a startling transformation. To contemplate what happens to a decaying corpse, as if this were the central point of *memento mori*, is actually a failure in our perspective. It is 'shooting short', and involves us in gazing at just 'The shells of fledge souls left behind', weeping as if this were all there is. The image is brilliant, as it combines the visual image of broken eggshells (a bit like the 'sticks' and 'Dry dust' of long-dead skeletons) with the conviction that these are no more than the evidence that something living has emerged and now flies free in a dimension we are unaware of. What we haven't taken into account erupts dramatically into the next stanza: 'since our Saviour's death did put some blood/ Into thy face:/ Thou art grown fair and full of grace'. The image is startling, given the previous talk about gaping skulls. The phrase about putting blood into someone's face is a homely expression beloved of solicitous mothers who seek to feed up their sons or daughters who may be grown up but are looking a bit peaky. And the comment about being 'fair and full of grace' might be a similar kind of comment about improved looks as a result of some healthy nourishment. Yet, of course, in each case there is a powerful double meaning about the significance of the Saviour's blood as the means of grace for the whole of creation. Herbert is the master of the pithy and everyday expression as a way of conveying profound religious insight. And rather than Donne's aggressive threat, 'Death, thou shalt die', he has a much gentler approach, suggesting that Death is to be loved and nurtured into a new form of beauty.

The last pair of stanzas responds to this extraordinary metamorphosis. Death itself is now like a living, breathing, resurrected person who is 'gay and glad' rather than uncouth and hideous. It is a vision of what the teaching about 'doomsday' will be: that is, the final day of reckoning and resurrection. Here, the poem's vision of death is more like Stanley Spencer's paintings that depict a general resurrection, with souls reunited with their bodies emerging from their graves in the ordinary churchyard at Cookham, yawning and stretching and greeting their neighbours in a happy way. As an exposition of what is meant in the creeds of the Church by 'the resurrection of the body', this poem is quite lovely: 'When souls shall wear their new array,/ And all thy bones with beauty shall be clad'. I must say that Herbert convinces me to feel much more comforted and hopeful, with this image of dressing up for a general celebration, than does Donne with his polemic against an adversary.

The thought in the last verse is not a new one. Once again, it is about feeling as safe lying down to die as we do to go to sleep. But it is expressed with a deceptive simplicity. 'Half that we have' is our dear body, now not despised or feared, but confidently expecting transformation. We are assured that we are moving towards 'an honest faithful grave', which will not betray our trust. And I love the idea of pillows that could be, interchangeably, 'either down, or dust'. What could be more comforting?

There Is a Place

There is a place prepared for little children,
those we once lived for, those we deeply mourn,
those who from play, from learning, and from laughter
cruelly were torn.

There is a place where hands which held ours tightly
now are released beyond all hurt and fear,
healed by that love which also feels our sorrow
tear after tear.

There is a place where all the lost potential
yields its full promise, finds its true intent;
silenced no more, young voices echo freely
as they were meant.

There is a place where God will hear our question,
suffer our anger, share our speechless grief,
gently repair the innocence of loving
and of belief.

Jesus, who bids us be like little children,
shields those our arms are yearning to embrace.
God will ensure that all are reunited:
there is a place.

John Bell and Graham Maule

Donne's poem (p. 145) speaks of all the places where death may lurk, including in the hands of 'desperate men'. In our generation in the developed world, we are largely unfamiliar with widespread infant mortality; for small children to die is exceptional, unless through human activity such as road traffic accidents, air crashes or deliberate domestic cruelty. But there is also a shocking phenomenon of 'school killings', where a disaffected loner enters a school building with the intention of slaughtering as many children as possible, and then turns the gun on himself. In Dunblane, Scotland, in 1996 such a massacre was enacted by Thomas Hamilton, who killed 16 five-year-old children and their teacher, also wounding many others. Since he held legal licences for the four guns he carried, the event gave rise to an immediate change in British

151

gun laws, effectively making the private ownership of hand guns illegal.

For the small town of Dunblane, and Scotland more generally, the event was beyond nightmare. Writing this song was the response of John Bell and Graham Maule, well known for their liturgical songs published by the Iona Community. In the face of such a tragedy, people's grief demanded to know what God was doing in all this, and what could be their hope for any kind of connection with their children beyond death. Where earlier generations of hymn writers confidently proclaim hope of eternal life, contemporary writers have been much less inclined to explore that area or make assertions about it. The authors, unusually, have chosen to address the urgent questions head on, and to articulate the promises that we can find some basis for in the Bible. Although the poem and its tune (named 'Dunblane') were written in a particular time of tragedy, the assertions could apply to the death of any child.

The poem is written with great simplicity, and with a gentleness that offers an unwavering comfort. Each stanza apart from the last repeats the promise, 'There is a place'. It echoes perhaps one of the few promises that the gospel shows Jesus making about what comes after this life: 'I go to prepare a place for you' (John 14.2). The first line may remind us of Victorian sentiments aimed at encouraging infant piety that in other circumstances we might find a little cloying: 'There is a place prepared for little children'. But as it proceeds, the agony of the parents is laid bare. The children, we discover, are already dead; they are 'those we once lived for'. What has been attacked is the activity children naturally engage in, and somewhere they should have been able to feel safe: play, learning and laughter. The place where the children lived turned out to be fraught with danger. The 'place prepared' is, by contrast, one of true and lasting safety.

The second stanza recalls what will be for parents one of the most vivid memories of their lost children – their grip of the adult's hand. In young childhood, the holding of hands is crucial, not just from love (and tiny children love holding hands, with adults and with each other), but in the endless vigilance required to keep a small and adventurous person safe. Keeping your child alive is the most basic task of parenthood; the parent of a dead child feels that they have failed in this fundamental way, even when they could have done nothing to prevent it. The promise of this verse is not only about release from fear for the children, but implies that there is sorrow in the heart of God, who shares the same love for the child and weeps the same tears as our own. This promise may recall Jesus' sayings about God, which start from the ordinary impulses of parenthood and argue how much more will God provide for his children (Luke 11.9–13).

The third stanza addresses the sheer sense of the loss of a future, of wasted potential that there might have been, had the children lived to be adults. It asserts that in some mysterious way there is a place where this loss is reversed and redeemed, and where the silencing of infant voices on earth is balanced by how they can 'echo freely/ as they were meant' in heaven. This is about a dimension of reality that it is impossible for us to conceive of from the perspective we now hold. This promise recalls that of the book of Revelation, where death shall be no more (21.4).

The fourth stanza addresses the almighty anger that is felt against a God who can allow such things to happen. There will be a place, an opportunity to hold God to account, almost as in a court of justice. 'God will hear our question,/ suffer our anger'. There are many places in the Bible where, rather than simply accepting that the ways of God must be just, the writer inveighs against God who permits injustice and does not appear to prevent innocent suffering or avenge it (Job 24.1–12).

The fifth stanza starts in a different way, with the name of Jesus, and his teaching that we ourselves must become 'like little children'. This asks us to identify with the children who died, as vulnerable but as lively and trusting as they were. It recalls the Gospel incident where Jesus is said to have let children come to him when everyone else was shooing them out of the way as unimportant (Mark 10.13–16). Only when we become like the unimportant ones do we find a way into the kingdom of God. The longed-for embrace that is denied us now will be redeemed when we join them, for we will also die in time.

The poem ends where it began: 'there is a place'. Not all of us may be able to believe in this promise. But it surely makes us cry with longing that it may be so.

There

There, in that other world, what waits for me?
What shall I find after that other birth?
No stormy, tossing, foaming, smiling sea,
   But a new earth.

No sun to mark the changing of the days,
No slow, soft falling of the alternate night,
No moon, no star, no light upon my ways,
   Only the Light.

No grey cathedral, wide and wondrous fair,
That I may tread, where all my fathers trod.
Nay, nay, my soul, no house of God is there,
   But only God.

Mary Coleridge

Mary Coleridge was the great-grand-niece of the poet Samuel Taylor Coleridge, and belonged to a family that was very well connected with the cream of the Victorian literary and artistic world, Tennyson and Browning being friends of the family. Coleridge was, at his request, working on a biography of the artist Holman Hunt when she died in her late forties of septicaemia following appendicitis. She was a linguist and published several popular novels as well as writing poetry. She did not marry and lived with her parents, but travelled to the continent each year and was no recluse.

This poem of wondering about the realm beyond death belongs in the 'Hope' rather than the 'Fears and fantasies' section of this book because of its tone of gentle assurance that all will be well – but also for its refusal to try to imagine, in any detail, what it is going to be like. It is interesting to compare with the poem by Charlotte Mew, 'In the Fields' (p. 7), which cannot envisage a lovelier world than this one, and for that reason gives less credence to the notion of one beyond it. Coleridge's poem similarly cannot really imagine heaven, and yet we do have the sense that she firmly believes it is there.

It is a brief poem with not a single unnecessary word. There is a reliable rhyme scheme (ABAB), and the pattern of each four-line stanza is regular, with three five-beat lines (iambic pentameter, beloved of Shakespeare and very suitable for English speech patterns).

Then each stanza is concluded with a two-beat line, which has the effect of 'replying' to the questions posed or the negative assertions made in the preceding lines. It feels like an 'orthodox' Christian interior debate, where ponderings about life and death are resolved with traditional promises and assurances. (These are largely found in the book of Revelation.) And yet the poem is much more subtle and interesting than that sounds.

Starting right in with what she is talking about, 'There, in that other world', she declares her own interest in 'what waits for me?' But the mood is gentle and wondering, rather than anxious or over-curious. The second question, 'What shall I find after that other birth?', makes it clear that there is no question in the speaker's mind as to whether or not there *is* another realm of being that she will be released into on her death. Calling it another 'birth', of course, echoes Jesus' words in John's Gospel, 'You must be born from above' (John 3.7). But seeing death itself as a process of inevitable new birth makes it a positive expectation (indeed the word 'death' is not used at all in the poem, though we are clear what she is talking about). However, we know that a newborn baby can barely open its eyes when it emerges from the womb, and there will be a great deal to take on and learn, which will only happen gradually.

The poem asserts the first of its evocative negative statements: 'No stormy, tossing, foaming, smiling sea,/ But a new earth'. The reference is to Revelation 21.1, where it is predicted that there will be no more sea, and there will be instead a new heaven and a new earth. The sea in the biblical period was identified with the realm of turbulence and evil. In the poem, it is not quite that. The adjectives describing the sea move from violent and threatening ('stormy, tossing') to really rather attractive and benign ('foaming, smiling'), almost mirroring the process of being born – a labour that starts in agony and ends in joy. The 'new earth', standing in its own line, gives an impression of stability after turbulence.

The second stanza is a whole series of negations, addressing our earthly experience of the variety of light and dark. The creation of light and its separation from darkness is, in the biblical account, the first act of creation. Here, the description of the light and dark that will *not* be 'There, in that other world' is poignant and beautiful, and points to the way in which we understand and make meaning of time passing. The seasons of the sun and the daylight 'mark the changing of the days'. The contrast and variety between light and dark offer the solace of 'the alternate night'. Without a night, there will also be 'No moon, no star, no light upon my ways'. This sets up a sense of loss, which is answered by the promise, 'Only the Light'. The reference here is Revelation 22.4, which asserts that God alone shall be their light. The poem recalls the quotation from Donne's sermon, 'no darkness nor dazzling but one equal light' (p. xiii). But the reader is very conscious of how loved and comforting is the familiar pattern of alternating light and darkness that we experience here.

The final stanza moves its gaze from the landscape of creation to the finest constructions of humanity seeking to worship God, which have provided sacred places for the speaker to be formed in her faith, like her ancestors before her. There will be 'No grey cathedral, wide and wondrous fair'. Again, there is some sense of regret or loss for what has been most inspiring on earth. But the speaker answers herself, in quite a motherly way, explaining what to expect as if to a child who has not quite grasped a grownup situation: 'Nay, nay, my soul, no house of God is there,/ But only God.' And so the series of negatives concludes very tenderly and comfortingly. Somehow the poem, which like the Charlotte Mew poem conveys vividly the sense of a loved earth that will be missed, manages, through nothing but negation, to imply a promise that can be trusted.

Hymn for the Mercy Seat

Wonder is what the angels' eyes hold, wonder:
The eyes of faith, too, unbelieving in the strangeness,
Looking on him who makes all being gift,
Whose overflowing holds, sustains,
Who sets what is in shape,
Here in the cradle, swaddled, homeless,
And here adored by the bright eyes of angels,
The great Lord recognised.

Sinai ablaze, the black pall rising,
Through it the horn's pitch, high, intolerable,
And I, I step across the mortal frontier
Into the feast safe in my Christ from slaughter.
Beyond that boundary all loss is mended,
The wilderness is filled, for he,
Broker between the litigants, stands in the breach,
Offers himself for peace.

Between the butchered thieves, the mercy seat, the healing,
The place for him to test death's costs,
Who powers his very killers' arms,
Drives in the nails that hold him, while he pays
The debt of brands torn from the bonfire,
Dues to his Father's law, the flames of justice
Bright for forgiveness now, administering
Liberty's contract

Soul, look. This is the place where all kings' monarch
Rested a corpse, the maker of our rest, and in
His stillness all things always move,
Within his buried silence.
Song for the lost, and life; wonder
For angels' straining eyes, God's flesh.
They praise together, they adore,
'To him', they shout, 'only to him'.

And I, while there is breath left to me,
Say, Thanksgiving, with a hundred thousand words,
Thanksgiving: that there is a God to worship,

There is an everlasting matter for my singing;
Who with the worst of us, in what
He shares with me, cried under tempting,
A child and powerless, the boundless
Living true God,

Flesh rots: instead, aflame, along with heaven's singers,
I shall pierce through the veil, into the land
Of infinite astonishment, the land
Of what was done at Calvary;
I shall look on what never can be seen, and still
Shall live, look on the one who died and who still lives
And shall; look in eternal jointure and communion,
Not to be parted.

I shall lift up the name that God
Sets out to be a mercy seat, a healing, and the veils,
And the imaginings and shrouds have gone, because
My soul stands now, his finished likeness,
Admitted now to share his secret, that his blood and hurt
Showed once, now I shall kiss the Son
And never turn away again. And never
Turn away.

Ann Griffiths, translated from the Welsh by Rowan Williams

This hymn by Ann Griffiths, here translated by Rowan Williams, is remarkable for its graphic and exultant vision of life beyond death, as the soul comes into the presence of God at the 'mercy seat'. This is the moment of judgement where, because of the sacrifice of Christ, the human soul will receive acceptance and mercy rather than condemnation. Griffiths is regarded as one of the foremost writers in Welsh, although her life was short, dying after childbirth in 1805 when she was only 29 years old. Initially rather dismissive of the Methodist revival movement in North Wales, after her mother died she was moved by an Easter Monday sermon, and at the age of 20 followed her brothers into the Methodist society. Her poetry is passionate and mystical, full of the assurance of the personal salvation that was so deeply sought by converts, and it reverberates with her thoroughgoing familiarity with the Bible.

The poem begins as if we are witnessing an extraordinary heavenly scene with 'The eyes of faith'. It is based on the Old Testament narrative about the ark of the covenant, which was regarded as deeply sacred, and was kept in a special tent with a curtained 'holy of holies' space within it. It was a chest containing the scrolls of the law, and had two golden cherubim with outspread wings shadowing a 'mercy seat', which was the empty place between them where the presence of God was thought to rest (Exodus 37.1–9). It was considered to be so holy that it was dangerous to approach; the priest had to put on special garments and perform sacrifices. One significant sacrifice was the dedication of a goat (the scapegoat) on which all the sins of the people were laid, which was then sent out into exile in the desert to atone for those sins (Leviticus 16).

Each stanza begins with an arresting image or invocation. Initially, the poem is all about contemplation, and starts with the expression on the faces of the angels: 'Wonder is what the angels' eyes hold'. Instead of trying to depict the face of God, she conveys its glory indirectly, through the gaze of the angels. That gaze is often referred to in Methodist hymns, and it is not only about passionate reverence; it is about incomprehension, *even* for heavenly beings, about the mystery they are worshipping. Christian faith asserts that the creator of all things took human flesh; it is an assertion that can never really make sense, even though it is vital for salvation. In this stanza, Griffiths describes the infinite power of God who is the source and sustainer of all that is in being; yet, through his 'overflowing', God came down to earth, becoming as vulnerable as it is possible to be, an infant 'swaddled, homeless'. This extraordinary paradox is what makes even the eyes of faith 'unbelieving in the strangeness'.

The second stanza steps back from the announcement of 'wonder' and recalls the moment of death. This is conveyed through images from the Old Testament, when the people of Israel were wandering in the desert. Mount Sinai is mentioned (where the Law was delivered to Moses), along with 'the black pall' (the cloudy pillar that led the people and hid God's presence), and the 'horn's pitch, high, intolerable' (the ram's horn trumpet that was commanded to be blown, Exodus 19). Other hymns also use passing through the desert as an image of passing through death – one thinks of 'Cwm Rhondda'. The poet speaks of stepping 'across the mortal frontier', which instantly makes her safe from slaughter, her wilderness filled. Then she introduces some legal images, in which Christ is a 'Broker between the litigants', standing in the breach between warring parties, or parties seeking to resolve a matter of justice.

And then it is revealed where precisely the mercy seat can be witnessed now. No longer in the space between the wings of the cherubim, it is in the place of greatest human savagery, 'Between the butchered thieves', namely on the cross of Christ, recorded in the Gospels as situated between two thieves who were also executed at the time of the crucifixion. So the possibility of mercy flows from the very point where Christ tested 'death's costs' due to the Law given at Sinai, as he himself becomes the scapegoat for the people's sins, going out 'Beyond that boundary' so that 'all loss is mended'. Again the paradox is insisted upon: the one who is being killed is the one 'Who powers his very killers' arms'. The image of the 'brands torn from the bonfire' refers both to the prophecy of Zechariah 3.2 and to the founder of Methodism, John Wesley. He was saved as a child from a burning house, and regarded himself as chosen by God for a special purpose. In the same way, forgiveness and cleansing are offered to all, as we too are plucked from the burning.

The fourth stanza, the centre of the poem, invokes the poet's soul (and ours) to pay attention: 'Soul, look'. Again, the paradox of faith, uniting utter helplessness and awesome power, is drawn out: 'This is the place where all kings' monarch/ Rested a corpse'. Christ's death and burial, his 'stillness' and his 'buried silence' nevertheless are the 'Song for the lost' and the fulcrum around which 'all things always move'. This gives way to the response of the speaker in the fifth stanza, with passionate thanksgiving 'while there is breath left to me' (we seem to be back in the land of the living, who have yet to die). The speaker rejoices that God himself has shared 'with the worst of us' what human life is like, and has 'cried under tempting' like herself (Hebrews 2.18).

The last two stanzas are in the form of a series of amazing promises to the speaker herself, and to all of us who have yet to die. Starkly stated, 'Flesh rots', and yet the promise of what lies beyond is glorious. Griffiths uses a series of vivid images: 'aflame' (Wesley spoke of his heart, at his conversion, being 'strangely warmed'); 'I shall pierce through the veil' (this recalls St Paul's mystical passages in 2 Corinthians 3.18); 'the land/ Of infinite astonishment'; 'I shall look on what never can be seen, and still/ Shall live' (witnessing that

God's mercy seat is no longer dangerous, but life-giving); 'in eternal jointure and communion' (the broken covenant has been restored).

The final verse once again takes up the idea of 'veils' that have been removed. This is a common theme in Griffiths' work, and she identifies 'imaginings' and 'shrouds' as the fantasies and speculations that are an inevitable condition of earthly human life, and divide her soul from the true understanding of her Saviour. The curtains of the holy of holies will be rent (Matthew 27.51), and God will remove the 'shroud' or 'pall' that hangs over all nations (Isaiah 25.7). St Paul reworks the image in his reflections on how faith will eventually be dissolved into knowledge, so that we may know even as we are fully known by God (1 Corinthians 13.12). 'And never turn away again': she is finally the creature God intended, 'his finished likeness', admitted to the astonishing intimacy of divine love.

That Nature is a Heraclitean Fire and of the comfort of the Resurrection

Cloud-puffball, torn tufts, tossed pillows ǀ flaunt forth, then chevy
    on an air-
built thoroughfare: heaven-roysterers, in gay-gangs ǀ they throng;
    they glitter in marches.
Down roughcast, down dazzling whitewash, ǀ wherever an elm arches,
Shivelights and shadowtackle in long ǀ lashes lace, lance, and pair.
Delightfully the bright wind boisterous ǀ ropes, wrestles, beats
    earth bare
Of yestertempest's creases; ǀ in pool and rut peel parches
Squandering ooze to squeezed ǀ dough, crust, dust; stanches, starches
Squadroned masks and manmarks ǀ treadmire toil there
Footfretted in it. Million-fuelèd, ǀ nature's bonfire burns on.
But quench her bonniest, dearest ǀ to her, her clearest-selvèd spark
Man, how fast his firedint, ǀ his mark on mind, is gone!
Both are in an unfathomable, all is in an enormous dark
Drowned. O pity and indig ǀ nation! Manshape, that shone
Sheer off, disseveral, a star, ǀ death blots black out; nor mark
           Is any of him at all so stark
But vastness blurs and time ǀ beats level. Enough! the Resurrection,
A heart's-clarion! Away grief's gasping, ǀ joyless days, dejection.
           Across my foundering deck shone
A beacon, an eternal beam. ǀ Flesh fade, and mortal trash
Fall to the residuary worm; ǀ world's wildfire, leave but ash:
           In a flash, at a trumpet crash,
I am all at once what Christ is, ǀ since he was what I am, and
This Jack, joke, poor potsherd, ǀ patch, matchwood, immortal diamond,
           Is immortal diamond.

Gerard Manley Hopkins

This initially very daunting and complex poem is in marked contrast with the previous one by Ann Griffiths, as it is located not in a vision of heaven but within an experience of the tempestuous but joyful buffetings of a particular kind of earthly landscape and weather. Apparently Hopkins wrote the poem directly after a walk on a bright but blustery July day following a storm, in a summer of almost continuous rain. As in many of his poems, he is clearly seeking to convey with both accuracy and passion some very distinctive observations of the natural world, blended with his deep Catholic convictions about the fate and direction of that world, and of his own place in time and eternity. In doing so, he takes what is basically a sonnet form (he himself referred to it as a sonnet), and wrenches it in a number of new directions, with a series of codas, as well as engaging in his usual creativity with new nouns and surprising grammar.

Perhaps we need to start with the curious title, surely one of the longest and most scholarly ever to put off the casual reader. Heraclitus was a pre-Socratic Greek philosopher whose words are only remembered in quotation by others. He understood that the world was in a state of permanent flux (his most famous statement is that all things flow, and that one can never step into the same river twice). He saw all the elements as engaged in a constant state of transformation into one another, but with fire as the most fundamental one ('all things are an interchange for fire, and fire for all things'). He seems to have rejoiced in paradox. Some scholars interpret Hopkins' poem as contrasting Heraclitean thought about continuous flow with Christian teaching about permanence and eternal hope. But I wonder if that is right? Some key Greek philosophers like Plato (who proposed certain and unchanging ideal Forms) argued against Heraclitus. And some Church Fathers, like Justin Martyr, saw both Heraclitus and Socrates as 'Christians before Christ'. I am not sure that Hopkins' title is really setting up an opposition, exactly.

I think the best way to begin to understand this poem is to try reading it out loud, and see what pictures and sounds it conjures in the imagination, through image and onomatopoeic sound. As you sound out the exultant wordplay, it becomes impossible to deny the poet's delight in and commitment to this infinitely shifting, variegated, beautiful earth. As I try to understand new words like 'chevy', 'Shivelights', 'shadowtackle', or puzzling constructions like 'in pool and rut peel parches', I am nevertheless caught up in the sense of being buffeted about by the wind that flings the glittering clouds around after a storm, and feeling how impossible it is to capture the ceaseless, writhing movements of elm branches in the boisterous breeze. There is a regular rhyme scheme, as in a traditional sonnet, but these rhymes feel like very frail guy ropes trying to anchor this exuberant poem to a form. The poet could be trying to give the reader a sense of that lively Heraclitean flow and mutual exchange and transformation. And he works with words, familiar and invented, in a way that bears comparison with the efforts in the visual arts of the Impressionists. Instead of painting the certain forms and lines we 'know' exist in our world, they attended carefully to what the human eye could actually see, and then tried to represent that. So the blotches and raw brushstrokes help to convey the impression of the world as it first comes to our senses, before we have interpreted it and fixed it into certainties. Just so with the depiction of the natural world in this poem, which is then summarized, as Heraclitus might have: 'Million-fuelèd, nature's bonfire burns on'.

At the centre of the poem is a meditation on the place of humanity in this ceaseless bonfire. This is quite poignant; it is as if somehow nature has an affection for 'her bonniest, dearest to her, her clearest-selvèd spark'. But in the natural world, however much humans try to make their mark, ultimately they are swallowed up and become irrelevant in the light of galactic time. 'Man' tries to contribute through his own little 'firedint' within the elemental conflagration of nature, but 'death blots black out; nor mark/ Is any of him at all so stark/ But vastness blurs and time beats level'. The thought here is similar to the famous poem by Shelley, 'Ozymandias', which mocks the pretensions of human figures of power who aspire to be remembered for ever, but are not ('The lone and level sands stretch far away').

These observations, in the light of growing contemporary know-ledge of the vastness of the universe and its age, are not wrong. But it is at this point that the poem suddenly announces 'Enough! the Resurrection,/ A heart's-clarion!'. At one level, this is a complete inter-ruption into what has gone before; it has not been led up to, except in the sense that in any Petrarchan sonnet the reader is expecting a significant twist or turn in direction. This is usually around the ninth line, but this sonnet has been lengthened and developed, so that the shift is delayed until the first of three codas to the form. It is almost as if the resurrection breaks in after an apparent gloomy ending, not only introducing a quite new reality and hope, but also influencing backwards our experience and perception of the earthly universe into which it bursts. And the exultation of this section about the resur-rection hope carries the same fast-paced tone and delight we felt in the first part of the poem. Things seem to fall out, not in a calm, normal pattern of living and dying, but in an apocalyptic tumble of events that echo each other: 'Flesh fade, and mortal trash/ Fall to the residuary worm; world's wildfire, leave but ash:/ In a flash, at a trumpet crash'. The general resurrection, heralded by the last trump (1 Corinthians 15.52), takes place back in the body on this intimate and lovely earth, and not in some Platonic realm of ideas. It is an answer to human grief or fear of death: 'Away grief's gasping, joyless days, dejection'.

The final two and a half lines are a statement of classic Christian belief, but I don't think they function as any kind of rejection of the delicious, exhilarating, destructive and creative natural world of the poem so far. That world has simply, as in this poem, been broken into by the act of God in taking human flesh, an act that renders every particular, frail human being capable not of leaving his own 'firedint', but of being heated and crystallized into a diamond, which will endure even in the heart of the fire: 'I am all at once what Christ is, since he was what I am, and/ This Jack, joke, poor potsherd, patch, matchwood, immortal diamond,/ Is immortal diamond.'

being to timelessness

being to timelessness as it's to time,
love did no more begin than love will end;
where nothing is to breathe to stroll to swim
love is the air the ocean and the land

(do lovers suffer?all divinities
proudly descending put on deathful flesh:
are lovers glad?only their smallest joy's
a universe emerging from a wish)

love is the voice under all silences,
the hope which has no opposite in fear;
the strength so strong mere force is feebleness:
the truth more first than sun more last than star

– do lovers love?why then to heaven with hell.
Whatever sages say and fools,all's well

E. E. Cummings

E. E. Cummings, a US citizen who lived from 1894 to 1962, saw two world wars and was active in the ambulance brigade in France during 1914–18. This gave him an enduring love of Paris and he returned often. He was raised as a Unitarian, and much of his poetry contains a sense of transcendence, as well as often a passionate eroticism. Much of his poetry explores the theme of death. The characteristic liberties he took with grammar, punctuation and the lack of capitalization often combine with his subject matter to convey a sense of awe, and an inability to capture or pin down the mystery of his theme. Somehow he manages to convey simultaneous playfulness and deep significance.

This poem about love that transcends death was written only a few years before his own death. It is a classic Shakespearean sonnet (see pp. 52–3), with three quatrains having half-rhymes (ABAB CDCD EFEF), followed by a couplet with firm full rhymes as a conclusion. The poem is an extraordinarily strong assertion of the certainty of enduring love, based, it seems, on our human experience of loving and being passionately loved.

The subject of the first quatrain is love itself. The assertion is that love has the same relationship to 'timelessness' as it has to 'time', which means not only that it will endure for ever, but that it had no beginning; it partakes of the nature of eternity. This is a huge claim – not one that is made of the universe itself, but only of God, who is traditionally seen as the Alpha and the Omega, incorporating all beginnings and endings because not subject to any of them. Any human relationship must of necessity have a beginning (through giving birth or experiencing a first meeting) and an ending (through the death of one of the lovers). But the boldness of this poem is to imply that any real love partakes of eternity through its quality (as in that familiar feeling lovers have that they have always known one another). Certainly, lines three and four return to locating love firmly on this earth, between those who are engaging in companionable physical activities ('to breathe to stroll to swim'). Here, love is the very atmosphere and landscape: 'love is the air the ocean and the land'. It is not that human love is endowed here with an impossible weight of significance. It's just that there is no part of the reality of this ordinary human experience that does not dwell in the reality of love that holds us in being.

The second quatrain is held within a long parenthesis. Cummings often uses brackets, almost as if whispering an aside, and yet they tend to contain material of significance. This sequence is made up of two questions and their answers: 'do lovers suffer?'; 'are lovers glad?' They could be regarded as rhetorical questions; where erotic passion is involved, as we all know, of course they do, and of course they are. And yet these tender and absurd questions provoke answers that stretch their significance much more widely. The remark about suffering, that 'all divinities/ proudly descending put on deathful flesh', is fascinating. It could be referring to the pagan gods of Greece and Rome, who were said to fall in love with human beings and were persuaded to appear in earthly form to woo them. (However, it was usually only the human side of that arrangement, or the resulting offspring, that ended up suffering.) It could be hinting at the Christian belief in the Incarnation and Passion of Christ. Or it could be just pointing out that all human passion, however exalted in its own self-estimation, always comes down to bodies in the end. The point is, though, that love always puts on 'deathful flesh'; the only kind of love we know about inhabits human bodies that are themselves subject to mortality.

The third quatrain is stunning, as a piece of assurance in the face of the death that we will certainly come to. Love is not just stronger than death: it is a continuing voice beneath all the silences we may feel, in grief or in our contemplation of creation; it is the kind of hope that has no anxious counterpart in terror; it has an enduring strength that makes mere violence seem feeble; and, again, it has neither beginning nor end. Once again, the poem earths what could sound abstract by putting 'truth' with physical bodies like 'sun' and 'star'.

The final quatrain, which deals in what we may believe about death, again poses an absurd 'rhetorical' question: '– do lovers love?' And without delay, without even a punctuation space before the next word, 'why then to heaven with hell'. This ironic inversion of the common dismissive phrase 'to hell with' manages in a light-hearted way to dump the concept of hell altogether. There is nothing to fear of judgement beyond death, because 'lovers love'; we know they do, and as the poem says as its final word, 'all's well'. We are reminded of the words of Julian of Norwich, reflecting at depth on her vision of the crucified Christ: 'All shall be well, and all shall be well, and all manner of thing shall be well.' This poem asserts the same thing, in a tone of voice that is both flippant and utterly serious. 'Whatever sages say and fools' suggests a tone of voice that is just brushing aside anyone else's views. But considered slowly, it covers the range of gloomy philosophizing, punitive religious teachings on hell, and just ordinary foolish human fear. Love is something we may truly rely on and rest in, in this life and beyond.

The Covenant and Confidence of Faith

Now it belongs not to my care,
   Whether I die or live:
To love and serve thee is my share:
   And this thy grace must give.

If death shall bruise this springing seed;
   Before it come to fruit;
The will with thee goes for the deed;
   Thy life was in the root.

If life be long, I will be glad,
   That I may long obey:
If short; yet why should I be sad,
   That shall have the same pay.

Christ leads me through no darker rooms
   Than he went through before:
He that into God's kingdom comes,
   Must enter by this door.

Come, Lord, when grace hath made me meet,
   Thy blessed face to see:
For if thy work on earth be sweet,
   What will thy glory be?

My knowledge of that life is small;
   The eye of faith is dim:
But it's enough that Christ knows all;
   And I shall be with him.

Richard Baxter

The calm and trusting tone of this hymn feels as if it comes from a core of serenity; but Richard Baxter lived and wrote in some of the most turbulent times in our history, experiencing the English Civil War and the restoration of the monarchy. A priest in the Church of England, he was Puritan and reformist by inclination, and acted at one time as the chaplain to one of Cromwell's regiments. However, he was not wholly convinced about this choice, and when the monarchy was restored, he was for a while a chaplain to Charles II. It is said of Baxter that he was too Puritan for the Bishops, and too

Episcopalian for the Presbyterians. When he was offered the bishopric of Hereford, though, he turned it down, and after a great number of dissenters had been ejected from their pulpits, and the Act of Uniformity passed, he retired as a Church of England priest, later taking out a licence as a Nonconformist minister. His views led him into trouble; at the age of 70 he was arraigned before the infamous Judge Jefferies for the crime of making a paraphrase of the New Testament, then fined, whipped and imprisoned for 18 months. The judge called him 'an old rogue, a hypocritical villain, a fanatical dog and a snivelling Presbyterian'. (These days he is remembered in the Church of England's official calendar of saintly people.)

Baxter's verse was published initially in 1681 as *Poetical Fragments: Heart Imployment with God and Itself; The Concordant Discord of a Broken-healed Heart*. This poem was written in memory of his wife Margaret, after her death from a lingering illness. He wrote beneath it, 'This Covenant my dear Wife in her former Sickness subscribed with a Cheerful will.' Initially having eight verses of eight lines each, the poem has been adapted in various ways as a hymn, since it uses simple language and a regular metre. I have retained most of the usual omissions, but ensured that all the text that appears is original; in this form it is a concentrated and remarkable meditation on death and what lies beyond it.

The language is simple and the tone serene, but the assertions of this poem are in no way banal; rather, they come over as the hard-won fruit of a lifetime of intense spiritual work, in response to both grace and difficulties. The first word of this extract, which is in hymnbooks normally rendered 'Lord', was originally written as 'Now'. It suggests a hinterland of spiritual struggle that has brought the speaker to this place of balance and acceptance. The first two lines could potentially be read as a statement of someone in grief who does not care about his life, but I think not. For it echoes the declaration of St Paul, 'whether we live or whether we die, we are the Lord's' (Romans 14.8). So perhaps when he speaks of 'my share' there is some emphasis on the word 'my'; the date of his death is not for him to worry about; his role is only to love and serve God whatever. There is a delightful edge to the last line of this verse, with the word 'must' making a logical requirement of God. He will not need to worry whether grace will be given him to focus on the love and service; it will, that's God's job.

The second verse addresses the force and action of death upon human intentions for their lives. In Baxter's era, the huge majority of people were cut down by death at an age we would regard as terribly young, if they attained adulthood at all – certainly at an age when we would expect still to have significant work and achievements ahead of us. Without modern medicine, almost every kind of illness and affliction had the potential to be deadly or crippling (Baxter himself endured periods of enforced rest because of great weariness). The imagery here is of damage to tender plants, denying them their fruiting stage. But the assurance is that what really matters – the presence and knowledge of God – 'was in the root'; whether or not a good work was completed is not the point with God.

The third stanza continues this theme, affirming obedience, whatever the length of years to be served on this earth. The final line, which may appear oddly mercenary, is usually revised in hymn books, but it makes perfect sense to those familiar with Jesus' parable of the labourers in the vineyard (Matthew 20.1–16). This tells the story of the master who employs casual labourers throughout a day, and then decides to give the same wage to all, whether they have worked all day under a hot sun or have only laboured for an hour. God is generous rather than fair, and gives us what we need rather than what we deserve. The story was often applied to varying lengths of human life, which have an equal prospect of heaven.

Without actually mentioning the fear of death, the fourth stanza addresses it gently. The image of being led through a series of dark rooms is an interesting variation on the 'valley of the shadow of death' (Psalm 23.4) – perhaps the image is suggested by the 'door' that we are coming to at the end. The assertion is implicit that Christ saves us precisely by having already gone through death himself, so there is nothing about the process that is unknown to God. When we are accompanying a dying person whom we love, it is painfully clear that we are not on the same path as that person is, and that we cannot follow where he or she is bound to go. But there is no separation from Christ in death. The last two lines are taken from the saying of Jesus in John's Gospel about himself as the Good Shepherd who guards the door of the sheepfold; he himself is the door through which all the sheep must come in (John 10.1–6). But here it is applied to death itself. There is no entry into heaven except through death.

The last two verses eschew any sort of speculation about what lies beyond death; indeed, they are very sparing. The speaker simply puts into God's hands the date of his death, based on when grace shall have made him 'meet' (ready, worthy) to see God face to face. There is then only an imaginative leap from the sweetness of doing God's work on earth to what the infinitely greater joys must be within the scope of God's glory in heaven. But then the poem reverts to the admission of an appropriate ignorance about what it can possibly be like – 'The eye of faith is dim'. Indeed. Only in Christ is there full knowledge; what we can trust in is the intimacy of his love: 'And I shall be with him'.

Let Evening Come

Let the light of late afternoon
shine through chinks in the barn, moving
up the bales as the sun moves down.

Let the cricket take up chafing
as a woman takes up her needles
and her yarn. Let evening come.

Let dew collect on the hoe abandoned
in long grass. Let the stars appear
and the moon disclose her silver horn.

Let the fox go back to its sandy den.
Let the wind die down. Let the shed
go black inside. Let evening come.

To the bottle in the ditch, to the scoop
in the oats, to air in the lung
let evening come.

Let it come, as it will, and don't
be afraid. God does not leave us
comfortless, so let evening come.

Jane Kenyon

Jane Kenyon was a remarkable poet and translator who battled with depression all her adult life and died of a virulent form of leukaemia at the age of only 47 in 1995. She grew up in the Midwest but married and moved to Eagle Pond Farm in New Hampshire, and her poems arise from a very strong sense of being rooted in a local, rural place. Her poetry is often religious, but it is spare with explicitly Christian references. It tends to be calm, luminous and completely lacking in self-pity. It has been said of her work that she 'sees this world as a kind of threshold through which we enter God's wonder'. When she died she was New Hampshire's poet laureate.

'Let Evening Come' gave its title to one of her poetry collections, published in 1990 (before her diagnosis). I have chosen it as the poem to conclude this anthology because it can be read either as a poem facing approaching inevitable death or old age with serenity and acceptance, or as one that celebrates continuing daily life, with its gradual, comfortable shifts between light and dark, and its regular rhythm of work and rest in a place of peaceful, ordinary beauty. It isn't necessary to choose between these readings. The poem is shaped as six brief stanzas, each with three lines. It is conversational, which is appropriate to a time of day when it is good to slow down and take a rest, and there are no rhymes.

Placing the reader with great immediacy in the farmyard that gives rise to its reflections, the poem is tissued with the invitation to 'let' things happen, whether it is the coming of evening, the movement of the sunlight or the habitual behaviour of people and other creatures at a certain time of day. So it has an immensely peaceful, almost lulling tone; whatever may be the anxieties or strivings we bring to the poem, it has the capacity to soothe without ever straying into the banal. It is as if the speaker of the poem is sitting on the verandah of the farmhouse, taking up her knitting and letting the light gradually change and fade as the day passes into night.

The poet works with great precision in the images she chooses to convey the time of day. The poem begins in late afternoon, which is captured by the exact way the low sunlight strikes the hay bales 'through chinks in the barn', moving up the bales gradually as the sun sinks in the western sky. It is interesting that at this stage of the poem, we are watching the sun moving upwards, rather than the shadows growing. Later on, we will reach the point where night is truly falling: 'Let the shed/ go black inside'. Instead of describing the sunlight directly, we see its impact on the objects that surround human life in this working, homely environment. It is for humans to accept the diurnal rhythm and let ourselves be affected by it, fitting in our work and rest appropriately.

The second stanza makes a lovely parallel between the evening call of the cricket, which chafes its long legs to make that familiar clicking sound, and the knitting woman who 'takes up her needles/ and her yarn'. The shape of the long needles echoes the powerful legs of the cricket, and both produce a comforting, rhythmic murmur. 'Let evening come'; in the hands of an experienced knitter, the activity is an evening job because it can be done in fading light, while sitting down.

The next three stanzas seem to be about details around the farm that the woman on the verandah can see or imagine around her as the light fades. She remembers (or notices) the 'hoe abandoned/

in long grass' – perhaps indicating a task to continue with tomorrow, but which cannot be done now. Now we are invited to 'Let the stars appear' – we are not just to put down our tasks but to allow the whole of creation to do what it always does and impinge on our awareness. It is not easy to describe the stars or the new moon in original ways, and the poet is very sparing here. Just the word 'disclose' in relation to the moon is distinctive. It is as if the heavenly bodies are waiting on our attention in order to reveal themselves.

Perhaps she sees a fox slinking past, and imagines its den. The wind dies down (this word is the only explicit hint that the poem could be a metaphor for death). But then the shed goes 'black inside'. Even when we notice the sun setting attentively, there is a shock of sudden shadow and cool when the sunset is complete. Even when we know that someone we love is dying, or that notionally we ourselves will die one day, there is a suddenness about the imminence of actual death. Yet we need to recognize and allow it: 'Let evening come'.

The penultimate verse varies the speech pattern and focuses on what the evening comes to. Of course, it comes to us as mortal human beings, but the poem says this indirectly, highlighting once again things that can be noticed around this particular farmyard. By this stage, the objects may be almost in shadow, unless they are glinting slightly in the moonlight that picks them out. There is the 'bottle in the ditch' – presumably some overlooked rubbish, but implying human behaviour, a refreshing drink enjoyed earlier. There is 'the scoop/ in the oats', which would have been used to measure out food for the animals around the farm. And there is 'air in the lung' – the breathing human body that senses the growing coolness. Eventually, evening will come to this body in the shape of death, and the breath of life will stop.

The last stanza is a gentle reassurance, which nevertheless does not let us pretend that we are immortal: 'Let it come, as it will, and don't/ be afraid'. As the coming of the dark may be fearful to a child, so we need to be comforted about the approach of our death. 'God does not leave us/ comfortless' is an echo of John's Gospel (14.18), where Jesus says, 'I will not leave you desolate; I will come to you.' It is, finally, all right to 'let evening come'.

Acknowledgements

———•●•———

R. V. Bailey, '(VII) Familiar', from *The Losing Game*, Mariscat Press, 2010.

John L. Bell and Graham Maule, 'There Is a Place', from *The Last Journey*, Wild Goose Publications, 1996. Copyright © 1996 Wild Goose Resource Group (WGRG), c/o The Iona Community, Glasgow G2 3DH, Scotland. Reproduced by permission, www.wgrg.co.uk.

Raymond Carver, 'What the Doctor Said', from *All of Us*, by Raymond Carver, published by Harvill Secker, 1996, reprinted by permission of The Random House Group Limited.

Charles Causley, 'Death of a Poet', from *Collected Poems*, Macmillan, 1992.

Gillian Clarke, 'Plums', from *Selected Poems*, Carcanet Press, 1985, and 'The Plumber', from *Ice*, Carcanet Press, 2012.

Billy Collins, 'The Art of Drowning', from *The Art of Drowning*, by Billy Collins, © 1995. Reprinted by permission of the University of Pittsburgh Press.

David Constantine, 'Common and Particular', from *Collected Poems*, Bloodaxe Books, 2004. Reproduced by permission or Bloodaxe Books, www.blood axebooks.com.

Jim Cotter, 'On Our Familiar Strand', from *Cancer Psalms*, by Jim Cotter, published by Cairns Publications. © Jim Cotter, 2012. Used by permission. rights@hymnsam.co.uk.

E. E. Cummings, 'being to timelessness as it's to time'. Copyright 1950, © 1978, 1991 by the Trustees for the E. E. Cummings Trust, from *Complete Poems: 1904–1962* by E. E. Cummings, edited by George J. Firmage. Used by permission of Liveright Publishing Corporation.

Ann Drysdale, 'Winter Camping', in *Between Dryden and Duffy: Another Collection, Poems by Ann Drysdale*, Peterloo Poets, 2005. Used by permission of the author.

Emily Dickinson, 'I heard a fly buzz when I died', reprinted by permission of the publishers and the Trustees of Amherst College from *The Poems of Emily Dickinson*, edited by Thomas H. Johnson, Cambridge, Mass.: The Belknap Press of Harvard University Press, copyright © 1951, 1955 by the President and Fellows of Harvard College. Copyright © renewed 1979, 1983 by the President and Fellows of Harvard College.

Copyright © 1914, 1918, 1919, 1924, 1929, 1930, 1932, 1935, 1937, 1942, by Martha Dickinson Bianchi. Copyright © 1952, 1957, 1958, 1963, 1965, by Mary L. Hampson.

Carol Ann Duffy, 'Wish', from *Feminine Gospels*, Picador, 2002. Copyright © Carol Ann Duffy, 2002.

U. A. Fanthorpe, 'The Unprofessionals', from *New and Collected Poems*, Enitharmon Press, 2010. © R. V. Bailey.

Ann Griffiths, 'Hymn for the Mercy Seat', translated from the Welsh by Rowan Williams, in *The Poems of Rowan Williams*, Carcanet Press, 2014. Reproduced by permission of Carcanet Press.

Kerry Hardie, 'She Replies to Carmel's Letter', from *Selected Poems*, Gallery Press, 2011. By kind permission of the author and The Gallery Press, Loughcrew, Oldcastle, County Meath, Ireland.

Seamus Heaney, 'Clearances III', from *Opened Ground, Poems 1966–1996*, Faber & Faber Ltd, 1998.

Elizabeth Jennings, 'Into the Hour', from *The Collected Poems*, Carcanet Press, 1986.

Jane Kenyon, 'Reading Aloud to My Father' and 'Let Evening Come', from *Collected Poems*. Copyright © 2005 by The Estate of Jane Kenyon. Reprinted with the permission of The Permissions Company, Inc. on behalf of Graywolf Press, www.graywolfpress.org.

Philip Larkin, 'Aubade' and 'An Arundel Tomb', from *The Complete Poems*, edited by Archie Burnett, Faber & Faber Ltd, 2012.

Denise Levertov, 'The Change', from *New Selected Poems*, Bloodaxe, 2003, reprinted by permission of Pollinger Limited on behalf of the Estate of Denise Levertov.

Roger McGough, 'Sad Music', from *Everyday Eclipses* by Roger McGough, © 2002, Viking – Penguin Books Ltd. 'I am not Sleeping', from *The Awkward Age* by Roger McGough, reprinted by permission of Peters Fraser and Dunlop (www.petersfraserdunlop.com) on behalf of Roger McGough.

Sasha Moorsom, 'Jewels in My Hand', from *Your Head in Mine*, Carcanet Press, 1994.

Kathleen Raine, 'Ah, God, I may not hate', from *Collected Poems 1935–1980*, George Allen & Unwin, 1981. Reproduced by permission of the literary Estate of Kathleen Raine, © 2000.

A. K. Ramanujan, 'A Hindu to His Body', from *The Striders*, Oxford University Press, 1966. Reproduced by permission of Oxford University Press.

Anne Stevenson, 'The Minister', from *Poems 1955–2005*, Bloodaxe Books, 2005. Reproduced with permission of Bloodaxe Books, www.bloodaxe books.com.

Acknowledgements

Dylan Thomas, 'Fern Hill' and 'Do not go gentle into that good night', from *The Collected Poems of Dylan Thomas: The Centenary Collection*, Weidenfeld & Nicolson, 2014.

All biblical quotations are taken from the Revised Standard Version of the Bible, copyright © 1946, 1952, and 1971 by the Division of Christian Education of the National Council of the Churches of Christ in the USA. Used by permission. All rights reserved.

My grateful thanks are due to Dr Jill Robson, Nicky Woods and Bishop Tim Stevens, who read and commented on my draft.

Printed and bound by CPI Group (UK) Ltd, Croydon, CR0 4YY

02/11/2023

08160004-0003